S0-ARD-251

1003 01 469428 01 1   (IC=1
FISHER, TIMOTHY.   04/30/81
HAMMOCKS, HASSOCKS HIDEAWAYS
(0) C1980 .   J 745.593

SONOMA COUNTY
LIBRARY

OFFICIAL
DISCARD

03

HAMMOCKS, HASSOCKS AND HIDEAWAYS

HAMMOCKS,
HASSOCKS

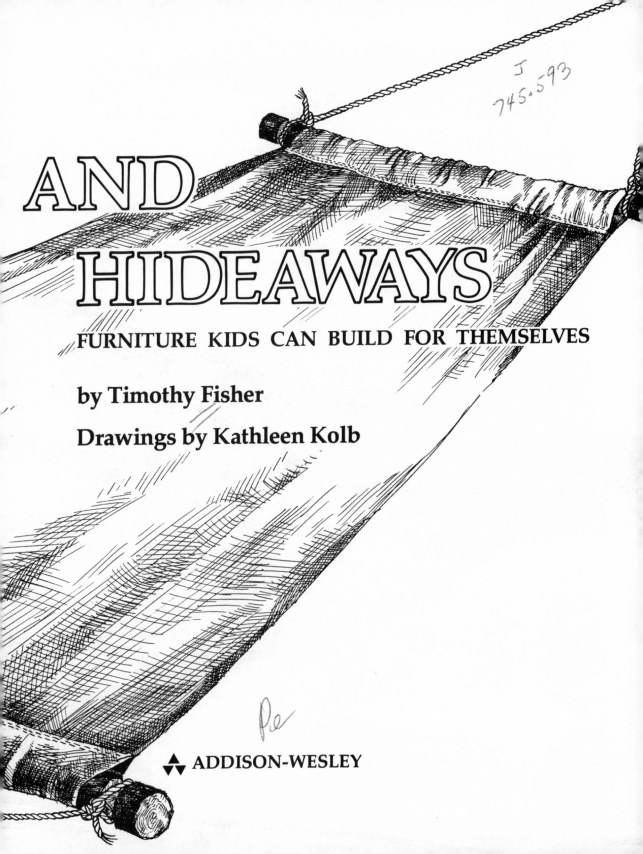

J
745.593

AND
HIDEAWAYS

FURNITURE KIDS CAN BUILD FOR THEMSELVES

by Timothy Fisher

Drawings by Kathleen Kolb

▲ ADDISON-WESLEY

Text Copyright © 1980 by Timothy Fisher
Illustrations Copyright © 1980 by Kathleen Kolb
All Rights Reserved
Addison-Wesley Publishing Company, Inc.
Reading, Massachusetts 01867
Printed in the United States of America
ABCDEFGHIJ-DO-89876543210

Library of Congress Cataloging in Publication Data

Fisher, Timothy.
  Hammocks, hassocks & hideaways.

  SUMMARY: Instructions for making various items of
furniture, such as chairs, desks, shelves, lampshades,
etc., from easily available materials.
  1. Handicraft—Juvenile literature.   [1. Handicraft.
2. Furniture] I. Kolb, Kathleen. II. Title.
TT160.F54   745.59′3   79-24812
ISBN 0-201-02936-7
ISBN 0-201-02938-3 pbk.

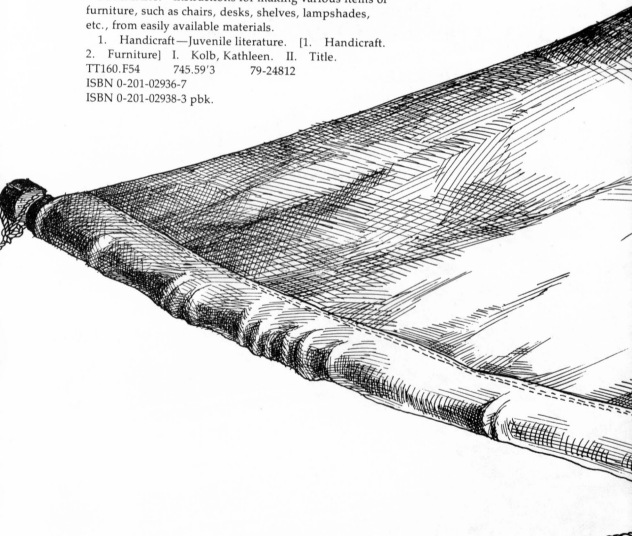

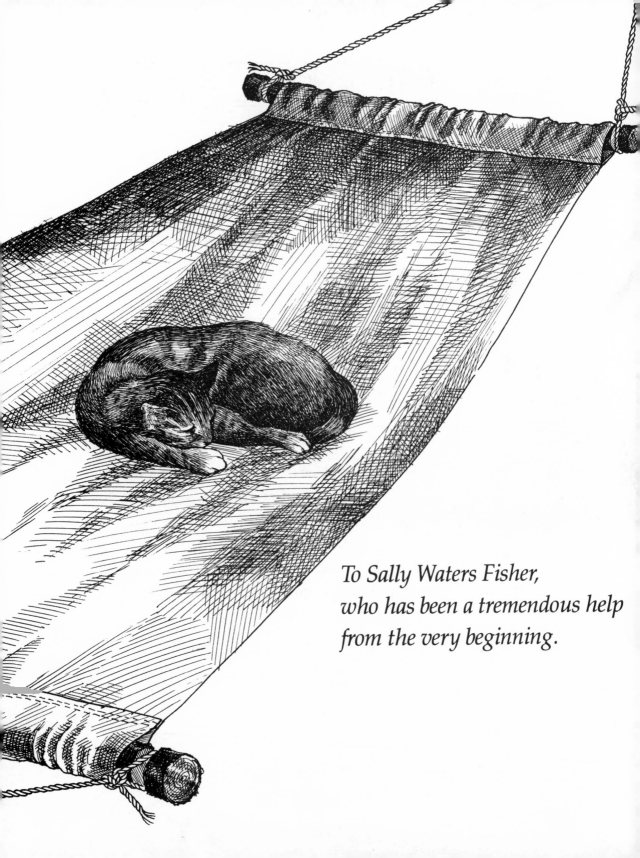

To Sally Waters Fisher,
who has been a tremendous help
from the very beginning.

CONTENTS

INTRODUCTION

If you've been looking for a way to make your own surroundings comfortable and private, one of the best methods is to build furniture yourself. While I was growing up, I experimented with hanging chairs and secret drawers and ways to divide and protect my room from the intrusion of my three brothers. I was fortunate in having access to the family tool box and sewing machine. To maintain this privilege I was careful of the tools and to consult my brothers or parents before I used their building materials. Before casually attaching any hardware or furniture to the floors, walls, or ceilings of your room, house, or apartment, remember that buildings are often more fragile and their owners more temperamental than one might wish; ask permission.

Here, as in my earlier book, HUTS, HOVELS & HOUSES, I've chosen materials that are easy to find, cheap, and often available free to the industrious scavenger. I've given specific instructions for each project, but I hope you'll use your ingenuity in substituting materials, changing the size and design of projects to meet your specific needs, and combining different elements of all the projects in new ways.

All the projects in this book can be built using only hand tools, though, naturally, power tools can be quicker in some situations, especially when it comes to sewing. We don't always think of the sewing machine as a power tool, but it is.

The more conventional types of furniture and construction methods are not included here. You probably already have such things as a bed, a bureau, and a straight chair. If you decide you want to get into building these standard items, there are many good books available. I hope you'll experiment with the whole spectrum of techniques and materials and soon be designing furniture unique to your needs and personality.

TOOLS AND MATERIALS

HAMMER

Hammering may seem elementary, but it is a skill and requires practice. If you have trouble controlling the hammer, hold the handle closer to the head, thus increasing the chances of hitting the nail rather than your thumb. (As I write I look at my own thumb, blue from just such an accident.) When using the nail-pulling end of the hammer, you may have trouble pulling out the longer nails. Place a block of wood under the hammer head next to the nail to get better leverage and help the nails come out straighter.

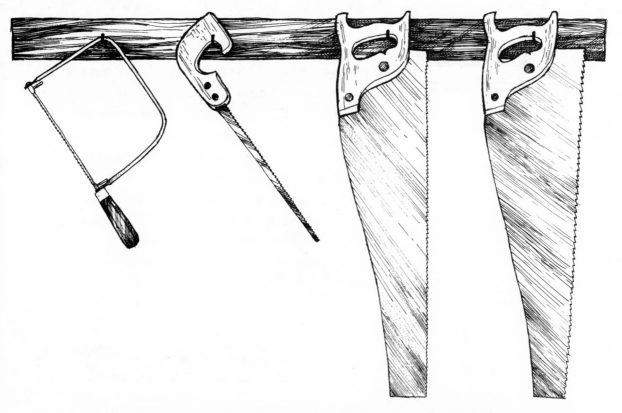

A *handsaw* cuts on the *down*stroke. Little force is required to cut with a sharp saw. You are mostly guiding the saw and gently pulling it up and down. The easiest error is to hold the saw at a slight angle, failing to make a square cut through the board.

A *keyhole saw* is a narrow, pointed saw, so named because it can actually fit through a keyhole. This is useful for cutting a hole out of the center of a board, for you can start from a drilled hole only about one-half inch in diameter.

A *scroll saw* (the motorized version is called a *jigsaw*) is a thin-blade handsaw for cutting curves or irregular designs.

A *ripsaw* is a coarse-toothed saw used for cutting wood in the direction of the grain.

SAWS

3

CHISEL

A wood chisel has a sharp cutting edge at one end and a handle at the other. You hold the chisel in one hand against the portion of wood to be removed. With your other hand, swing a hammer or mallet and tap the top of the chisel handle. Don't hammer too deeply or the chisel will get stuck. Remove a little wood at a time, working from opposite sides to chisel the hole deeper. Sharpen the chisel frequently. Never use it as a pry bar or screwdriver, please.

A square is used to measure a line at a 90-degree angle to another line. A 90-degree angle is also called a right angle, a perpendicular angle, or simply "square."

SQUARE

Unless otherwise indicated, it is assumed that any piece of lumber will be cut at a right angle. To draw a right angle on a board, hold one edge of the square against the edge of the board and draw a line on the board against the other edge of the square. To make one surface perpendicular to another, place the square at the junction of the two surfaces so they both rest directly against the perpendicular edges of the square.

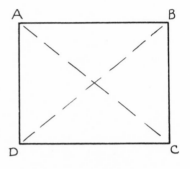

When constructing a square or rectangular shape, remember that distances between two sets of diagonal corners should be equal. As shown in the diagram, the distance between A and C will be equal to the distance between B and D. This is a good way to check the accuracy of your angles and measurements.

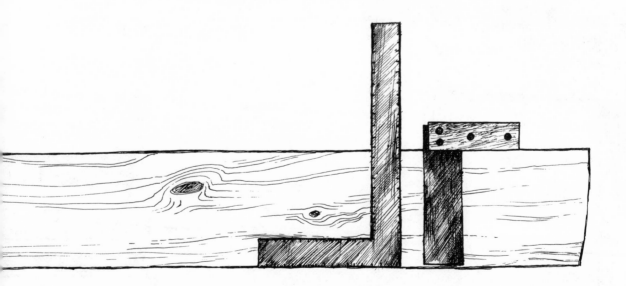

SEWING MACHINE

The one power tool most useful to these projects is a sewing machine. A power saw or drill will save a little time, but sewing by machine is a large savings compared to hand sewing. Hand sewing will certainly do the job, however.

The seams or sewed portions of furniture in this book have to take a lot of stress, so it is important that they are strong. Use heavy thread and double stitch.

I begin many of the sewing projects by telling you to *hem* the edges of a piece of cloth. To do this, double the cloth over twice and stitch it down so that no raw edges are exposed. This protects the fabric from fraying and gives it a tidy edge.

A 2 × 4 (called a *"two-by-four"*) is a piece of lumber 2 inches thick and 4 inches wide. Likewise a 2 × 6 is 2 inches thick and 6 inches wide. The term 2 × 4 indicates the rough-sawed dimensions of the lumber. In planing lumber, however, a small amount of wood is shaved off on each side, so that although they still *call* it a 2 × 4, its actual dimensions are less. You will have to calculate for this discrepancy when following the measurements in the projects using planed lumber. Often I will refer to a board by its *planed* dimensions, such as ¾- by 3½-inch, rather than the 1 × 4 it was sold as.

LUMBER

PAPIER-MACHÉ

Papier-maché is moldable paper saturated with paste. When dry it is light and strong.

A number of projects in this book require papier-maché. It is also good for making puppets, masks, and sculpture, so you may have already discovered it in an art class. Usually you put papier-maché over a framework such as wood, wire, cardboard, a balloon, or clay.

I recommend using wheat paste in papier-maché. It is sold inexpensively as wallpaper paste at hardware stores. Mix the wheat paste with water to a thicker-than-cream consistency. If the mixture is too thick, you will have difficulty saturating your paper.

Take newspaper strips about 2 inches wide and 6 inches long. Dip them into the paste so that they are totally wet, but not oozing, and spread them across your framework. You will want at least three full layers of papier-maché for adequate strength.

You can use paper towels rather than newspaper for more detailed work. For still finer details, use toilet paper. Drop about a foot of toilet paper at a time into a pot of paste. Mix this up and repeat until you have added enough toilet paper to make a thick moldable mush. Build up the fine details with this paper mush and let it dry.

8

Papier-maché will sometimes dry in a day, but it may take longer depending on the thickness, humidity, and temperature. Place it near dry heat to speed the drying process. Dry papier-maché will often have a rougher surface than when it is wet. If this disturbs you, you can sand the surface or fill in the wrinkles with wood putty. Hard papier-maché can be painted and varnished to give it some water resistance.

FINISHING

Most furniture will benefit from some sanding, oiling, painting, or varnishing. When sanding, it often works well to wrap your piece of sandpaper around a block of wood small enough to fit comfortably in your hand.

Begin with a coarse-grade sandpaper on your sanding block. After you have been over all the rough surfaces with the coarse paper, sand the furniture with a medium-grade, then a fine-grade sandpaper. Always try to keep your sanding motions in the *same direction as the wood grain* or else you'll make visible scratch marks across the grain. When sanding endgrain or the edges of plywood, however, you can sand in any direction.

If there are any depressions in the wood surface, you can fill them with a wood putty. To make a filler similar to the color of the wood, mix a thick paste using sawdust of that wood and a little white glue, such as Elmer's. When dry, sand the filler flush with the wood or add more filler if necessary.

When using paint or varnish be sure you have a solvent with which to wash the brush promptly after it's used. A commercial paint thinner is cheap and efficient. Even a water-based paint should be washed from the brush with plenty of water and a little soap before it hardens.

Many paints work best if a primer or sealer is applied to the wood surface before painting. If you are building hardwood furniture, consider applying a natural linseed oil or other furniture oil finish, rather than a paint or varnish.

ON-THE-FLOOR-FURNITURE

INNER-TUBE HASSOCK

This hassock consists of a car-, truck- or tractor-tire inner tube inflated inside a cloth case. The inflated inner tube stretches the cloth case tightly across the donut hole part of the tube, making a comfortable hassock or cushion.

First, inflate the inner tube. Next spread two pieces of cloth at least as big as the innner tube on top of each other on the floor. Smooth the cloth so there are no wrinkles. Place the inner tube on the cloth and draw around it so that you have a circle the size of the tube's circumference.

Pin the pieces of cloth together and sew, following the circle. Leave one-eighth of the circle unsewn. You can sew either by hand or

machine, but be sure to make it strong; this
seam will be under a lot of tension. Leave a
1-inch border outside the stitching and cut off
any excess cloth. Turn the case inside out by
pulling the cloth through the one-eighth circumference opening. Deflate the inner tube and
lay it smoothly inside the cloth case. Reach
inside the case with an air pump and screw the
tube valve to the pump hose. Inflate the inner
tube until the cloth is stretched taut across the
top and bottom of the hassock. Reach inside the
case and unscrew the pump from the valve.
Finish your hassock by sewing the remaining
opening in the case by hand. Safety pins will
hold back the bulging inner tube as you sew.

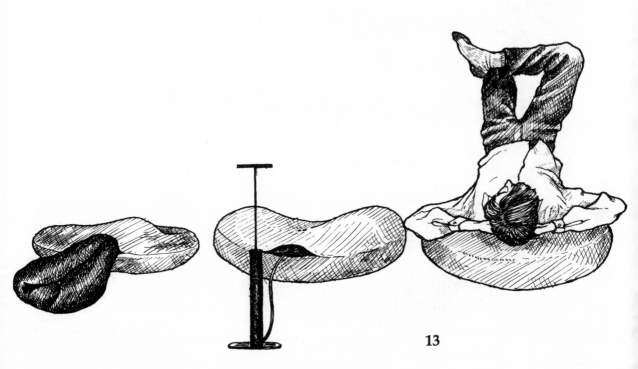

STUFFED SACK SEAT

This chair is nothing more than a big pillow. Nothing complicated, but comfort needn't be complicated.

Take a rectangle of cloth 1 yard wide and 2 yards long. Fold the cloth in half, forming a double-layered square. If it is patterned cloth, fold so that the pretty side is inside. (The pattern will show when turned inside out.) A few straight pins along the edges will help keep them lined up for the next step.

Now sew (a sewing machine is a big help) around all the sides of the square of doubled cloth, leaving only a 1-foot unsewed opening

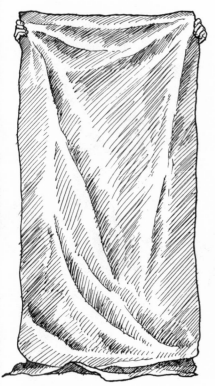

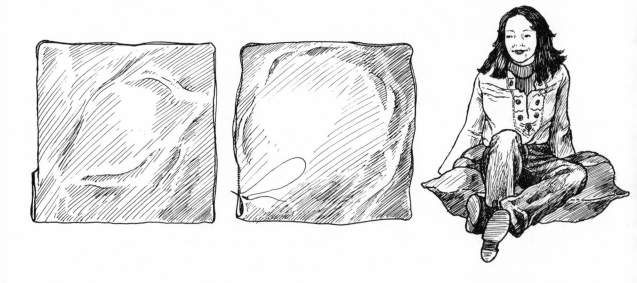

along one edge. Double stitch for added
strength.

    Turn this cloth sack inside out, so the
seams are on the inside. You are now ready to
stuff the chair. Small scraps of any soft material
are ideal. My favorite stuffings are ripped-up
scraps of foam rubber and /or the small styro-
foam pellets often seen in packing material.
Stuff the sack until it is full. Then, using strong
thread, sew up the 1-foot opening. Punch out a
depression in the center of the sack, sit back,
and relax.   **15**

RIGID-BOLSTER STUFFED CHAIR

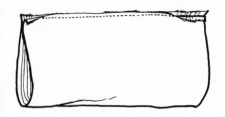

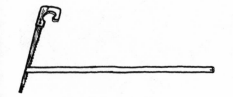

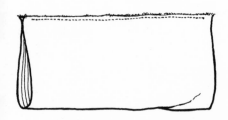

This chair consists of four dowel-centered, foam-rubber bolsters suspended between two side frames of plywood. Cut four 1-inch dowels (old broomsticks are fine) 26 inches long. Saw a 1-inch-deep slit through the center of both ends of each dowel. Get four 2- by 6-foot pieces of 1½-inch-thick foam rubber. Roll one piece of foam rubber tightly around each dowel. It should make a roll about 9 inches in diameter. You can substitute with foam rubber that isn't exactly 1½-inches thick; just make sure that the outside diameter of each bolster measures 9 inches. Tie or tape the foam temporarily in its roll until you get a case made.

The case for the bolster is a tube of cloth with a drawstring on each end to hold the foam rubber securely around the dowel. Use a fabric you like. You will need 3⅜ yards of 36-inch-wide cloth, or 2 yards of 60-inch-wide cloth. Either way, cut four 30- by 36-inch pieces of cloth.

To make each bolster case, fold one 30- by 36-inch cloth in half lengthwise with the right side inside. (The *right* side refers to the better-looking side of a piece of cloth, such as a printed pattern or the soft surface of corduroy or velvet.) The folded-in-half cloth will now measure 15 by 36 inches. A few straight pins will secure it as you stitch along the long edge opposite the fold, leaving a ¾-inch seam allowance. *Stitch only to within 2½ inches of each end.* Turn the tube inside out.

At each end of your seam, fold in the unstitched ¾-inch seam allowance along the

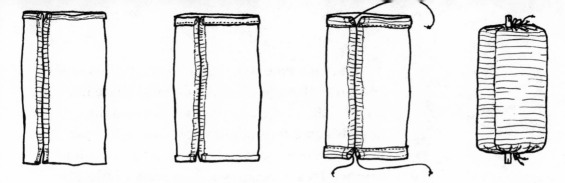

seam line. Baste it with several large stitches to hold it in place.

Next fold ½ inch to the inside on each open end. Iron or stitch this fold. Now make a second fold to the inside, 1 inch from the first fold, and pin it in place with straight pins. This will be your casing for the drawstring. Starting at one end, stitch the casing down next to the first fold as shown in the diagram.

Using a large safety pin, thread a yard of twine or nylon cord through each casing. Stuff the bolster, dowel and all, into the case and pull the drawstrings tight, tying them around the dowel. Repeat this process for the three remaining bolsters.

To make the sides of the chair, measure and cut two 25- by 23-inch rectangles of ¾-inch plywood. Saw out a 21- by 5-inch piece from each of these. On one of your pieces of plywood, mark out the lines and distances shown in the diagram. Place the marked piece of plywood directly on top of the other piece of plywood and hold them tightly in place using clamps or twine. Drill a 1-inch-diameter hole through both pieces of plywood in the four designated spots. If you want to paint or varnish the chair sides, it is easier to do it now, before the pieces are assembled.

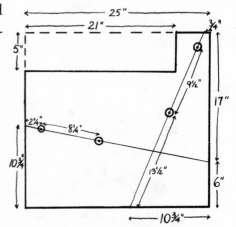

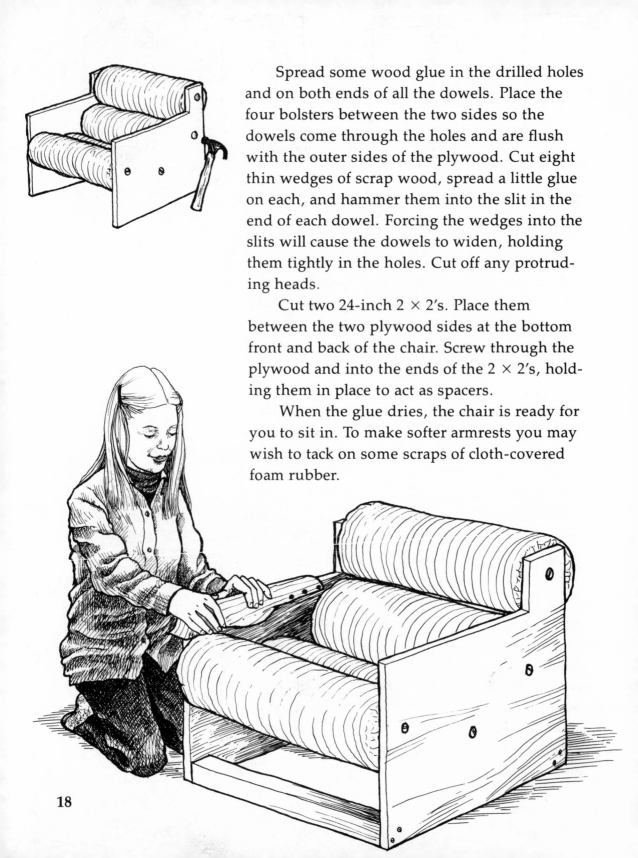

Spread some wood glue in the drilled holes and on both ends of all the dowels. Place the four bolsters between the two sides so the dowels come through the holes and are flush with the outer sides of the plywood. Cut eight thin wedges of scrap wood, spread a little glue on each, and hammer them into the slit in the end of each dowel. Forcing the wedges into the slits will cause the dowels to widen, holding them tightly in the holes. Cut off any protruding heads.

Cut two 24-inch 2 × 2's. Place them between the two plywood sides at the bottom front and back of the chair. Screw through the plywood and into the ends of the 2 × 2's, holding them in place to act as spacers.

When the glue dries, the chair is ready for you to sit in. To make softer armrests you may wish to tack on some scraps of cloth-covered foam rubber.

This chair is a glamourless stack of corrugated cardboard, but it's comfortable, and except for the glue, it's free for the scavenging.

Cut a 30- by 30-inch square of cardboard using a utility knife against a metal straightedge. (Cut on a scrap piece of wood or cardboard so as not to scratch the floor or table.) Spread a thin layer of white glue (like Elmer's) on top of the cardboard and stack another piece of the same size on top of the first. Continue stacking and gluing until you've made a 16-inch-high stack. Except for the bottom and top, it's not necessary that all the cardboard pieces be the full 30- by 30-inch size. Each layer can be a patchwork of equal-thickness pieces.

CORRUGATED CHAIR

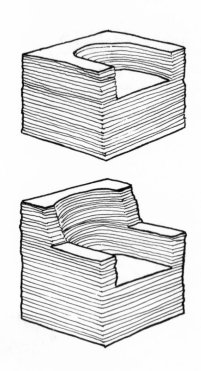

For added strength alternate the direction of the corrugations in each layer.

To make an armrest/backrest section, cut U-shaped pieces of the same 30- by 30-inch outside dimensions, but with a comfortably rounded 17- by 20-inch section removed for the seat. Stack and glue these U shapes to a height of 7 inches. The interior size of the back of the U's should be enlarged slightly with each layer to give the backrest a comfortable angle.

Continue stacking cardboard only behind the backrest area for an additional 8 inches.

To refine the finished chair, even the edges of all the layers with a handsaw and a rasp. Add cushions for extra comfort.

This desk consists of a flat top supported at each corner by a 28-inch section of fiber tube. (These tubes are used as disposable forms to make pillars out of poured concrete.) Fiber tube usually comes in 12-foot lengths and is available at a building supply store. If you can't find scrap tube and have to buy a whole 12-foot tube, don't panic. You can use leftovers for other projects in this book.

Measure a 10-inch-diameter tube into four 28-inch lengths. Mark off 28 inches from the end of the tube in at least four spots around the circumference. Line up an ordinary handsaw between your marks and saw through the tube. *This must be done accurately.* If the cut is not at a 90-degree angle to the tube, it won't stand up straight. If the cut is uneven, the tube won't rest flat on the floor or against the desk top.

FIBER-TUBE DESK

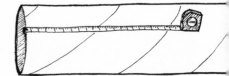

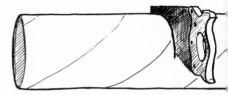

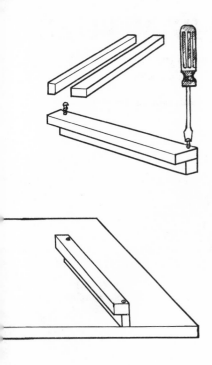

Your desk top can be made from a smooth-surfaced door, plywood, or boards nailed together with braces underneath. Place a tube under each corner and the desk is finished.

A plastic dishpan makes a good drawer. To hang the dishpan from the desk you will need two brackets that will fit under the rim of the dishpan. Cut two 15-inch-long ¾- by 1-inch wood strips and two 15-inch-long ¾- by ½-inch wood strips. Using 2-inch screws, screw the narrower strips to the wider ones. These screws will extend through each bracket and into the underside of the desk top. Place the brackets parallel to each other, spaced so that their protruding edges fit under the dishpan rims. This dishpan drawer should slide easily on the brackets.

Cardboard tubes can be used to support benches or tables of different heights. Your scrap pieces of tube could also support a shelf under part of your desk.

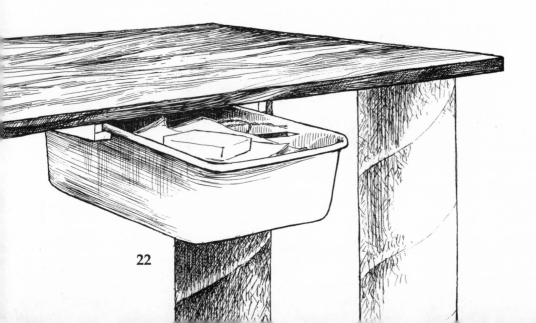

To make this desk into a snazzy dressing table, thumbtack a cloth skirt around the edges of the top to enclose the underside of the table. Place the dressing table against a wall. For a movie-star makeup mirror, hang a mirror on the wall behind the dressing table and string white Christmas-tree bulbs around the ege or frame of the mirror. Use U-nails or tape to hold the wires in place. Hammer the U-nails *only partially* into the wall or mirror frame; if hammered in too far, they could cut into the electrical cord. And for safety's sake, don't plug in the lights while attaching them to the mirror.

DRESSING TABLE WITH MOVIE-STAR MIRROR

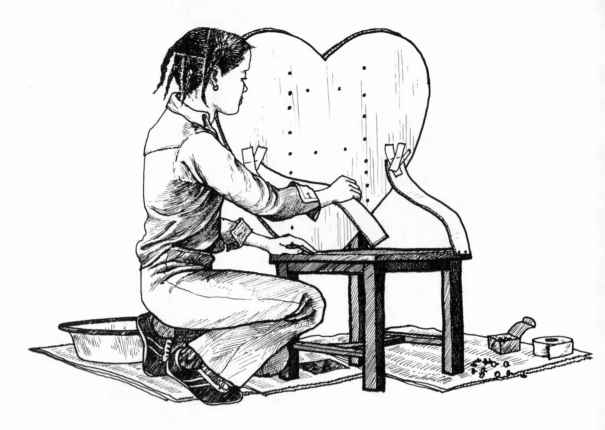

THRONE

Starting with a simple straight chair you can build your own throne.

With small nails and tape, attach pieces of cardboard to the chair to build a high back and armrests for your throne. Then cover the throne with several layers of papier-maché. (Consult the section on Tools and Materials, p. 8, for papier-maché directions.)

There are many possible details you can build into your throne. Consider such things as lions' feet or your personal coat-of-arms. You can paint the throne gold, and glue on marbles and mirror chips for jewels. You can attach elegant feather plumes above your head and sit on velvet cushions. Let your imagination be your guide.

24

Electric and telephone wire comes rolled on large wooden spools that are often discarded when the wire is used up. I've found you can make a good rocking chair from such a spool. The one I used was 26½ inches in diameter, but larger spools would work well, too.

The spool consists of two wooden circles connected by a central hub of 18½-inch-long, slightly curved boards. There are circular grooves on the inside of the two circles for the ends of these 18½-inch boards to fit into. Three long thin bolts pass through the hub between the two circles. These bolts hold the spool together by pulling the two circles tightly against the hub boards.

To make your chair, unthread the nuts on the ends of two of the bolts and pull the bolts out of the spool. You can then force the circles far enough apart to remove two-thirds of the hub boards. Leave boards only in the one-third of the hub circle between the remaining bolt and one of the holes from which you removed the other bolts. Now replace this second bolt and fasten tightly with its nut.

Sit inside the remaining one-third of the hub. You will use one of the removed 18½-inch hub boards as a backrest. Judge from sitting in it where a comfortable position for a backrest would be. Hold a hub board in that position and mark around the ends of it on the inside of the two circles. Following your marks, chisel a groove out of each circle to hold the backrest board. (Make your grooves the same depth as the hub grooves that originally held the board.)

CABLE-SPOOL ROCKER

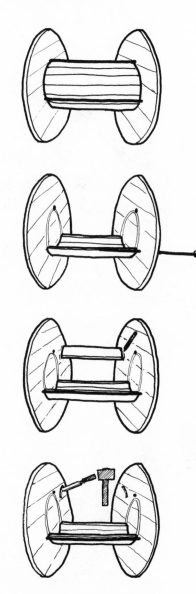

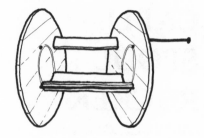

Fit the backrest into position. Drill a hole to fit the remaining bolt through both circles at a point just behind the backrest. Thread the bolt through these holes and screw the nut tightly. The chair is ready to sit in. You may want a seat cushion.

If you are a wild rocker, you can nail a crossboard between the edges of the two side circles at a point that will keep the chair from rocking over backwards.

This is a piece of furniture with two uses: It serves as a stepladder to get to the top of a bunk bed, and it's also a six-shelf bedside table for occupants of both top and bottom bunks.

It is constructed from two 2 × 4 **A**'s with shelves between. You can make each **A** as follows:

Lay two 6-foot 2 × 4's next to each other on the floor with the 4-inch sides facing up. Mark off each foot on each 2 × 4. Move one end of the 2 × 4's 3 feet apart. Cut one 3-foot and one 10-inch 1 × 4. Temporarily nail the 3-foot 1 × 4 to the ends of the 2 × 4's as shown in the diagram. Nail the 10-inch 1 × 4 to join the 2 × 4's at the top of the **A.** There should be small triangular points of the 2 × 4's below the 3-foot 1 × 4 at the base of the **A.** Saw off these triangles so that when you stand the **A** up, its feet will rest flatly on the floor. Nail a 1 × 4 between the 2 × 4's below each 1-foot marked measure. This will create five parallel 1 × 4's between the top and the bottom 1 × 4's. The bottom 3-foot 1 × 4 can now be removed. Saw off any protruding ends of the 1 × 4's so that they are flush with the 2 × 4's.

LADDER-BEDSIDE TABLE FOR BUNK BEDS

You are now ready to connect the two **A**'s. Use 1-foot-long boards for the shelves. The front boards of the shelves will also serve as steps, so be certain they are sturdy. Place the 1-foot boards between the two **A**'s so that the boards rest upon the 1 × 4 cross braces. Nail the boards in place. Obviously your shelves will be deeper at the bottom of the **A**'s than at the top.

Nail a 6-foot 1 × 4 diagonally across the back of the shelves between the top of one **A** and the bottom of the other. This forms a diagonal brace that will give the ladder/shelves rigidity. Saw off any protruding ends of the 1 × 4. You can add sides or a back to any of the shelves.

IN-THE-AIR
FURNITURE

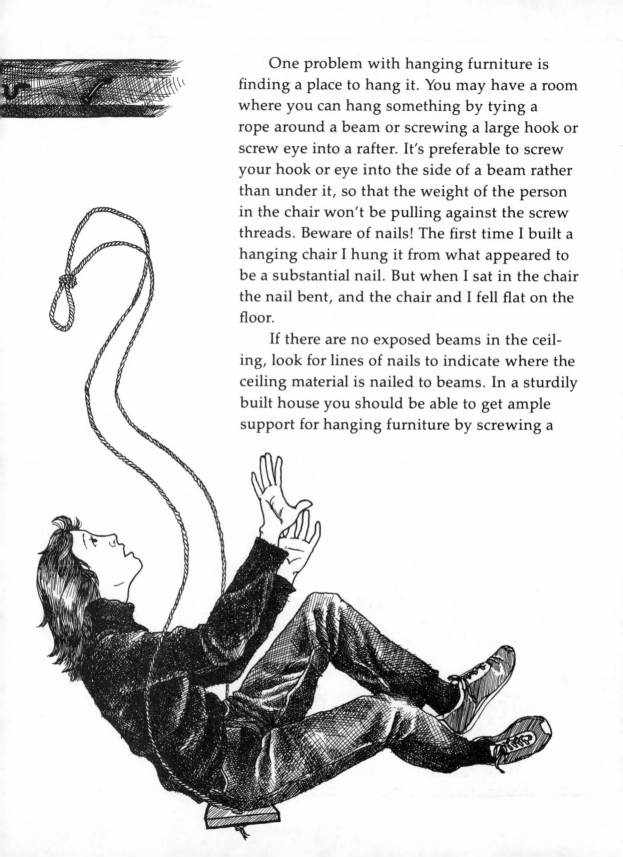

One problem with hanging furniture is finding a place to hang it. You may have a room where you can hang something by tying a rope around a beam or screwing a large hook or screw eye into a rafter. It's preferable to screw your hook or eye into the side of a beam rather than under it, so that the weight of the person in the chair won't be pulling against the screw threads. Beware of nails! The first time I built a hanging chair I hung it from what appeared to be a substantial nail. But when I sat in the chair the nail bent, and the chair and I fell flat on the floor.

If there are no exposed beams in the ceiling, look for lines of nails to indicate where the ceiling material is nailed to beams. In a sturdily built house you should be able to get ample support for hanging furniture by screwing a

large hook or screw eye through the ceiling into the beam. But don't casually start screwing hooks into the ceiling without the owner's permission and a pretty good idea of whether or not it can support the weight and stress of your hanging furniture. Door frames are also usually sturdy enough to support hanging furniture.

A simple **A**-frame can be built to hang furniture. Each **A** is built with two 7-foot 2 × 4's. Lay them out on the floor as shown in the diagram. Nail a 10-inch 2 × 4 between the 7-foot 2 × 4's, 6 inches below the top of the **A**. At the base of the **A**, nail a 4-foot 1 × 4 between the ends of the 7-foot 2 × 4's. Saw off the extra triangular stubs of the 2 × 4's so the **A** will rest squarely on the floor.

Nail the two **A**'s to opposite walls of the room. Nail a 2 × 6 between them, resting it on top of the 10-inch 2 × 4's at the tops of both **A**'s. Hang the furniture from the 2 ×6.

If all this sounds too complicated, just hang your furniture from a tree. **31**

CANVAS SLING CHAIR

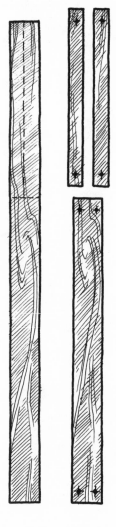

This is one of the most comfortable chairs I've ever sat in. It has a gentle motion that is a pleasant cross between a rocking chair and a swing. It consists of a long rectangle of canvas hung (just like a marionette) from wooden struts.

For the struts you can use a 5-foot planed 2 × 4. (Actual dimensions are about 1½ by 3½ inches.) Cut the 2 × 4 into one 22-inch and one 38-inch length. Take the 22-inch 2 × 4 and with a ripsaw rip it in half lengthwise into two approximately 1½- by 1¾-inch struts. If you buy the 2 × 4, you may be able to have it cut and ripped at the lumber yard. (This chair would be just as nice with struts made out of saplings or branches, if you can find some that have recently been pruned.)

Drill ⅝-inch diameter holes through both smaller struts at points centered 1½ inches in from each end. Drill two ⅝-inch diameter holes next to each other through each end of the 38-inch strut, centered on points 1½ inches in from the end and ¾ inch in from each side. Also drill a centered ⅝-inch hole through the middle of the 4-inch face of this wide strut. With a plane or knife and sandpaper, round and smooth all edges of the struts.

Hem a large piece of canvas into a rectangle 18 inches by 74 inches. Fold under both ends of the canvas in order to make casings to slip your smaller struts through. One casing requires an 8-inch fold and the other a 5-inch fold. Sew down the folds with lines of stitching 7½ inches and 4½ inches, respectively, in from and

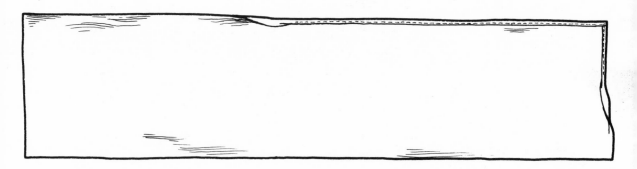

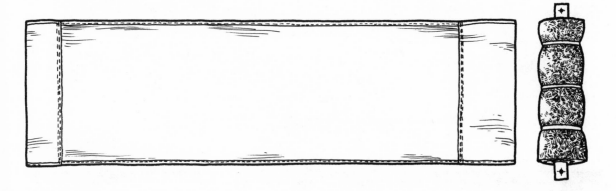

parallel to the folds. There will be a lot of strain on this stitching, so use strong thread and go over it at least twice.

Cut a 28- by 18-inch rectangle of ½-inch foam rubber or a shorter piece of thicker foam. Roll this foam tightly around one 1½- by 1¾-inch strut so that the foam roll just fits between the drilled holes. Wrap some tape or string around both ends of the roll to keep it rolled up. Insert this foam-wrapped strut through the 8-inch casing. Insert the 1½- by 1¾-inch strut through the 5-inch casing.

The last step is the rope rigging. Cut a 4-foot and a 10-foot length of ½-inch-diameter rope. You will start with the 38-inch strut and the 10-foot piece of rope. Thread the rope up through one hole and down through the one next to it, making both ends the same length. Thread one end of the rope through each hole in the foam-wrapped strut. Tie a knot in both ropes under this strut to maintain a distance of 44 inches between struts. Now at the back end of the 38-inch strut, feed the 4-foot rope up through one hole and down through the other. Thread one end of the rope through each hole in the remaining 1½- by 1¾-inch strut and tie

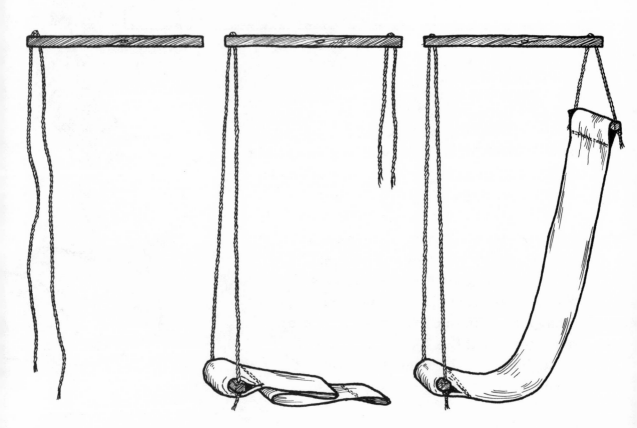

knots in the ends to maintain a distance of 15 inches between struts.

All that remains is the hanging. Measure another piece of ½-inch-diameter rope to the length you'll need where you plan to hang your chair and tie a knot in one end. Thread the rope through the hole in the middle of the 38-inch strut so that the knot rests under the strut. Tie the other end to whatever you want to hang from. Sit down, settle back, and swing.

35

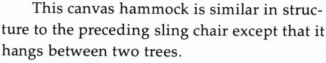

HAMMOCK

This canvas hammock is similar in structure to the preceding sling chair except that it hangs between two trees.

Buy a 9-foot length of 36-inch-wide canvas. Fold over ½ inch on each end of the cloth. Make another fold 5½ inches from the first fold and sew each end into a casing as for the sling chair. This leaves an 8- by 3-foot piece of canvas.

Look for some hardwood saplings (such as maple, ash, or oak) that average 2 inches in diameter, and cut two 4-foot lengths. These will act as spreaders to keep the canvas evenly separated. (Without spreaders the canvas scrunches you into a wad.) If you can find saplings with a slight curve in them, the hammock will be more comfortable. Two inches from each end of each spreader cut a notch ½ inch wide and ¼ inch deep all around.

Put one spreader inside each casing. Cut one 10-foot length of sturdy rope. At one end of the hammock tie one end of the rope around

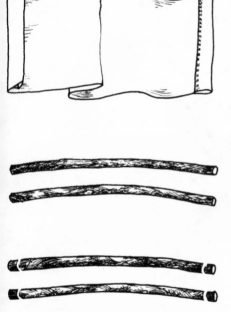

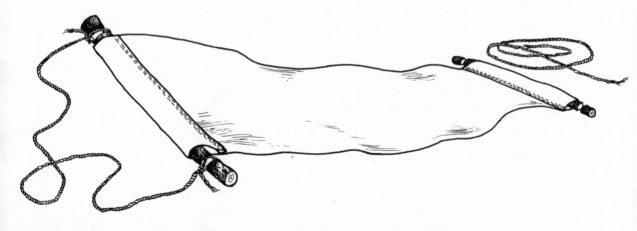

one of the notches in the spreader. Tie the other
end of the rope around the other notch in the
same spreader. Find the midpoint in the rope
and double it over itself at this point. Tie the
double rope into a knot, making a small loop.
Cut a second 10-foot length of rope and attach it
in the same manner to the spreader at the other
end of the hammock.

You can now hang the hammock by pass-
ing a piece of rope through each loop and tying
it around a tree. If you don't have two properly
spaced trees, tie the hammock between a tree or
post and a hook in the side of a building. It can
also be hung inside a large room.

I especially enjoy lying in my hammock
under the maple trees on a summer evening
looking out across the valley at the sunset. This
hammock is cozy for two people, too. You may
want to try making a wider hammock of similar
design.

TWIN ROPE-LADDER HANGING SHELVES

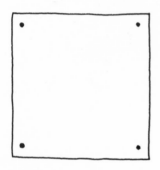

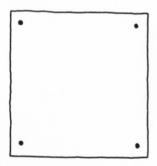

Hanging shelves make a midair table or storage shelves at any height and are particularly handy at the top of a bunk bed.

Cut three identical squares of ½-inch (or thicker) plywood. The plywood squares will be your shelves. They may be of any convenient size. I made mine 18 inches on a side. Place the three plywood shelves directly on top of one another and measure in 1½ inches from each corner. At each of these four points drill a ½-inch-diameter hole through all three shelves. If you want to paint the shelves, it is easier to do it now.

Select one piece of plywood for the bottom shelf. Thread a 10-foot piece of ⅜-inch rope through two adjacent corner holes in the bottom shelf. Adjust the rope so that equal lengths emerge from the holes on the top side of the shelf. Knot the rope ends tightly against the top of the shelf so the rope cannot move. Thread and knot another 10-foot piece of rope through the remaining two corner holes in the plywood shelf. You now have four rope ends coming up through each of the four corners of the bottom shelf. Tie another knot in each rope at a distance 1 foot above the shelf. Take a second shelf piece and thread one rope end through each corner hole so this shelf, held by the knots, will be suspended 1 foot above the bottom one.

Tie a third knot in each rope 1 foot above the second shelf. Thread the rope ends through the four corners of the top shelf so it will be suspended directly above the two lower shelves.

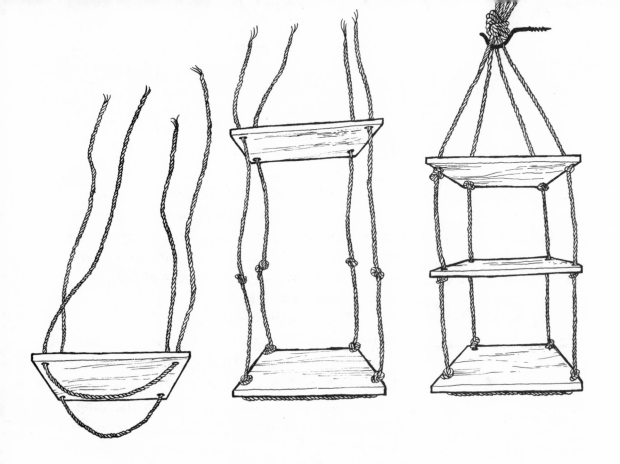

Pull the loose ends of rope with equal tension and tie all four of them together so that the knot is directly over the center of the shelves. You can hang the shelves from the ceiling by this knot. If you find that your shelves twirl around too much, you could hang them from two or even from four points.

You could, of course, have more than three shelves and vary the spacing. If you prefer sides on the shelves, boards can be nailed to the shelf bottoms or simply attached to the ropes with U-shaped nails.

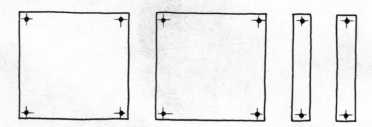

RIGID-BOTTOM HANGING CHAIR

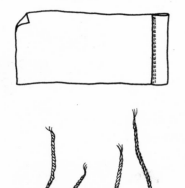

This uses essentially the same materials and principles as the hanging shelves. Your two ropes should be 14 feet long. You will also need two 18- by 20-inch pieces of ⅝-inch (or thicker) plywood. Cut two 18-inch lengths of 3-inch-wide boards for arm rests.

As in the shelf project, drill ½-inch-diameter holes 1½ inches in from each corner of the plywood pieces. Drill a centered hole 1½ inches from each end of the armrests.

You will need a piece of cloth for the sling backrest. Canvas, an old towel, or any sturdy cloth is fine. Hem the cloth to 22 by 9 inches. Fold over 1½ inches on each end of the cloth, leaving a 19- by 9-inch piece. (Pin the folded cloth to keep it in place while you sew.) Now sew down the folds with a line of double stitching, parallel to but 1½ inches from the fold line. This forms a casing at each end of the backrest to thread the ropes through.

You assemble this chair as you assembled the shelves. Thread the ropes under and through the bottom (seat) plywood. Knot the ropes in position. Tie a knot in each of the four ropes at a point 9 inches above the seat. Thread the rope through the two 18-inch armrest boards so they are 9 inches directly above the two 18-inch sides of the seat.

Decide which of the 20-inch edges will be the back of the chair. Take the two ropes that emerge from the armrests at that edge and thread one through each of the casings in the backrest. With the backrest in place, tie a knot in each of the four rope ends 4 feet from the seat. Thread the rope ends through the four corner holes in the other 18- by 20-inch piece of plywood so that it will be suspended 4 feet directly above the seat.

Pull the loose ends of rope with equal tension and tie them together so the knot is directly over the center of the seat. Use the rope extending above this knot to tie the chair to the rafter, tree branch, or whatever.

This is a very comfortable chair, but you may want a cushion on the plywood seat. You can build a scaled-down version of this hanging chair as a swing for a small child.

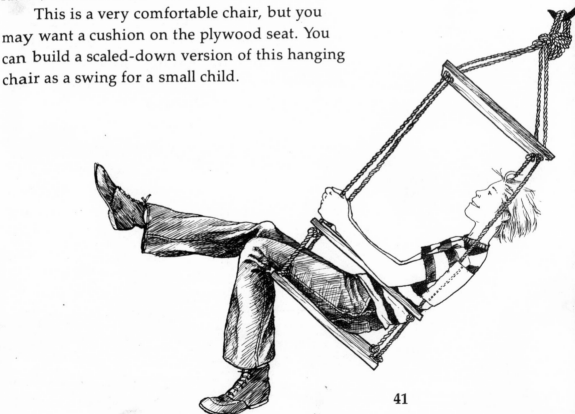

41

BLOCK-AND-TACKLE TABLE

This table gives you a large work space even if you have only a small or shared room. The whole table will pull up to the ceiling when you are not using it.

If you are in the middle of a project, game, or jigsaw puzzle, you won't have to disturb it or clean it up. Simply store it on the ceiling until you have time to continue. If you don't build this table now, think about it next time someone badgers you to pick up the mess you just barely got through making.

The basic table is a 4- by 8-foot sheet of ½-inch plywood. Cut six 10-inch 2 × 2's for legs. Stand one 2 × 2 under each corner of the plywood. Nail through the plywood and into each leg to hold the legs in position. Nail the two remaining legs under the center of the two 8-foot edges of the plywood.

Cut two 4-foot-long ¾- by 5½-inch planed boards and two 8-foot-1½-inch-long ¾- by 5½-inch planed boards. (These are sold as 1 × 6's.) These boards are nailed into the sides of the legs to hold the legs stable and provide a

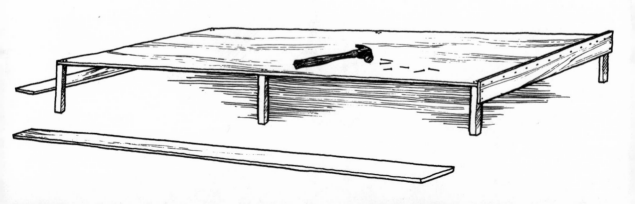

nice edge to the plywood. You have the option of attaching them either flush to the top edge of the table or in such a way that they extend an inch or so above the table top, making a rim all around. The rim will discourage materials from falling off the edges of the table (and hitting you on the head) when you pull it up to the ceiling. Nail the 4-foot boards to the 4-foot ends of the table, then nail the two 8-foot-1½-inch boards to the long sides of the table, overlapping the ends of the 4-foot boards.

Fasten a screw eye into the side of each corner of the table. Tie a piece of ⅛-inch-diameter nylon cord to each screw eye (the length will depend upon the height of your ceiling and size of your room). Place the table where you want it to be in the room. Screw a sturdy screw eye into the ceiling directly above each corner of the table. A pulley should be hung from each screw eye by a short piece of cord that will allow the pulley to pivot. Feed the nylon cord from each corner of the table through the pulley directly above it.

Exactly how the rigging of the rest of the ropes goes will depend upon the size and arrangement of your room. The trick is maintaining equal tension on the four cords so that the table raises and lowers evenly. At one edge of the ceiling hang a four-sheave pulley. (A *sheave* is the grooved wheel inside a pulley block.) If you can't buy a four-sheave pulley, hang two double-sheave pulleys next to each other. Feed the four ropes through this pulley, weigh down the table, and pull on all four cords with equal tension without lifting the table off the floor. Knot all the cords together at a point just beyond where they pass through the pulley. It will help to tie all four cords together in a few more spots below the four-sheave pulley. With the cords tied together, they will move as a unit, thus keeping the table level as you raise it. Attach a hook or cleat to the wall of your room below the four-sheave pulley. This will bear a lot of weight and should be attached to a structural beam. Now you can pull on the knotted cords and raise the table to the ceiling. Tie or cleat the cord to the wall to keep the table up.

TAKE-APART
FURNITURE

HINGED LOCK-UP BOX

This is a locking box held together by tabs, hinges, and a padlock. It dismantles easily to fold flat.

Cut four 18- by 18-inch squares of ½-inch plywood. Take two of these squares and cut two 10- by ½-inch slots on opposite sides of each one, parallel to and 1½ inches in from the edges. A simple way to cut these slots is to drill a ½-inch hole at both ends of each slot and saw between them with a keyhole saw. Using three pairs of hinges, hinge these four squares together, alternating the slotted and plain squares as indicated in the diagram.

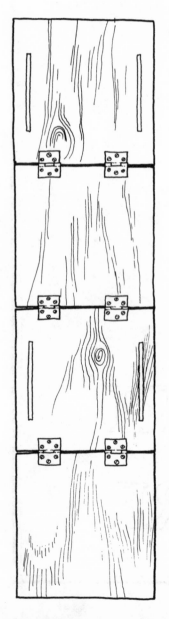

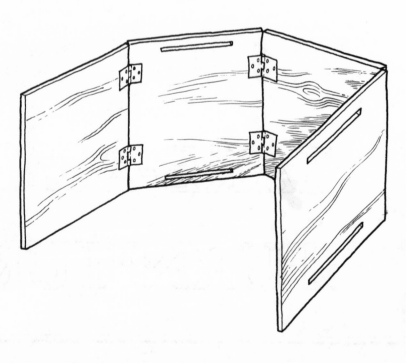

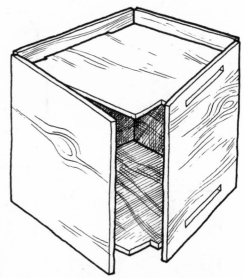

Cut two 18- by 20-inch rectangles of ½-inch plywood. Cut a 4- by 1-inch section from each corner, so that what remains is an 18-inch square with two 1- by 10-inch tabs protruding from opposite ends.

Assemble the box by folding the hinged pieces around the two tabbed pieces so the tabs fit into the slots. Attach a hasp to the unhinged corner. Add a padlock and the box is complete.

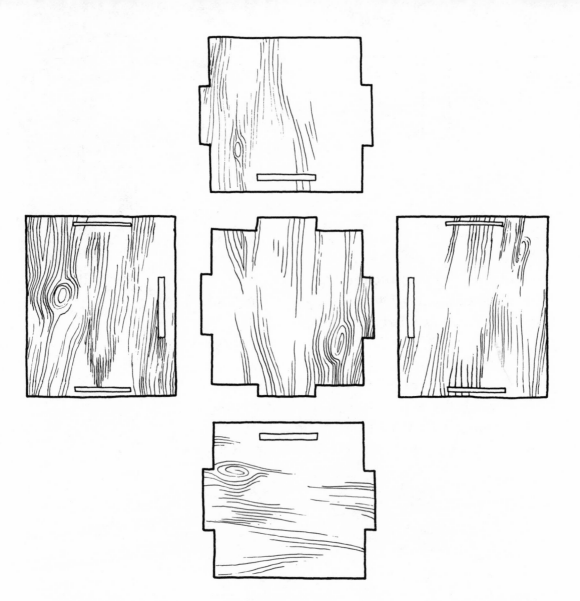

SLOT-AND-
TAB BOX

This is a completely collapsible box. It could be any size and made of plywood or sturdy (preferably double- or triple-layer) corrugated cardboard.

Cut the slots and tabs as indicated in the diagram. As in the previous project, the slots are as wide as the tabs are thick. It is probably

48

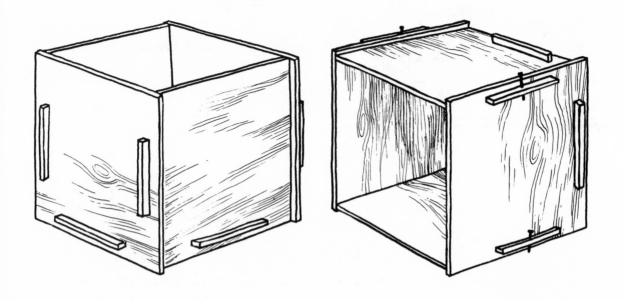

easier to make a cubelike box, but a rectangle isn't hard. Perhaps the best tactic is to make a model of your box out of thin cardboard (such as file cards) so you'll understand how it goes together. Note that the tabs extend through the slots far enough so that you can put a peg through the tab to hold it tightly in place. Two sides are made with three slots. The other two sides have two opposite tabs and a slot at the bottom, and the bottom piece has tabs on all four edges.

Assemble the box and drill a hole in each side tab to put a peg through. Make sure you drill the hole so that when the peg is in place, the tab will be pulled tightly through the slot. The pegs could be made of wood wedges, dowels, or nails. The sides should hold the box together well enough that you won't need pegs in the bottom tabs. **49**

TAKE-APART TABLE

You have probably noticed the cardboard dividers that separate the bottles inside liquor cartons. These separators are slotted together. We use a similar slotted effect to support this table. These dimensions are for a work table, but this design is equally applicable to a low table or stool.

The table can be made from one 4- by 8-foot sheet of plywood or composition board. Cut two 30- by 48-inch pieces of ⅝-inch plywood for the table base. You will have to cut a ⅝-inch-wide slot halfway through the center of both pieces of plywood as shown in the diagram. Use a chisel to cut off the end of the slots

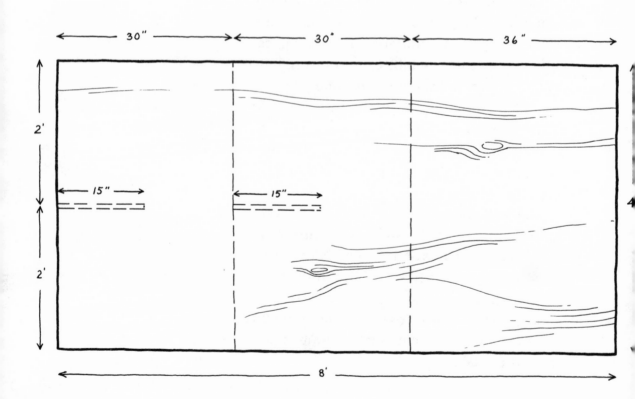

after sawing down the edges. Fit the slots into each other, making a 30-inch-high base that is X shaped when you look down on it.

For the top use a 3- by 3-foot or 3- by 4-foot piece of plywood (depending on whether you want a square or rectangular table). If you have other square or round materials, feel free to use them.

Cut eight 18-inch 1 × 1's. Turn the table upside down so the top is on the floor and the base is evenly positioned on top of it. Screw the 1 × 1 strips into the table top so that they fit tightly against all sides of the base.

The table can now be turned over and is ready for use yet easy to take apart. If the table gets moved around a lot, I suggest drilling a small hole in each of the four sets of 1 × 1's and the top edges of the plywood base. Then you can slip a nail through the strips and plywood to hold the top to the base. Finish your table by sanding the cut edges of the plywood and painting or varnishing it.

OUTDOOR FURNITURE

LASHING

Starting with only twine, a saw, and some sapling trees, you can lash together a bench in the woods.

Before attempting this bench, you should first try to find trees and branches that are "windfalls." If it is necessary to cut a tree or branches, be sure to get permission beforehand from the owner or forest ranger.

Locate two trees that have trunk diameters of approximately 10 inches and are growing about 3 to 5 feet apart. Find and cut two branches

or saplings 1½ to 2½ inches in diameter that are long enough to extend between the two trees and protrude slightly beyond them. At a height of 15 inches lash these poles between the two trees, one pole on each side of the trees. Wrap the string back and forth in every possible pattern. To make the lashing extra tight, wrap your last portion of twine around the lashing between each pole and tree and tie it securely.

Cut 18-inch-long sticks (1 to 1½ inches in diameter) for the seat. How many you need will depend on the diameter of your sticks and length of your bench. Lash one end of each

stick to one of the long poles until your bench stretches from one tree to the other. Then lash the other end of each stick to the other pole. If you want a backrest, simply lash a few more poles between the trees on one side of the bench seat.

You could make a table following these same procedures, except at a higher level. You could even try shelves.

FERRO-CEMENT

For outdoor permanent furniture, you can't beat ferro-cement. (You may not be able to lift it, either). Ferro-cement is cement mortar reinforced with steel. In this case our steel is in the form of chicken wire. It is surprisingly easy to make a bench using only scrap boards, used window screen and chicken wire, some sand, and less than one bag of cement.

When I started this project, I intended to make only a simple short bench, but it was too tempting to add a long neck (which also serves as a backrest) and a head, so it became an animal-bench.

You can use really junky lumber for this project because it all gets covered with wire and mortar. Once the mortar is dry the ferro-cement provides the strength of the bench. The wood structure could rot away and not affect your furniture.

Using approximately 1 × 5 lumber, cut two boards 24 inches long for sides, two boards 14 inches long for bench ends, and four boards 17 inches long for legs. Nail a 17-inch leg at a right angle to each end of each 24-inch board, creating two broad U-shapes. Nail the two U-shapes to the 14-inch boards and you have what looks like a topless bench or low table. The wire and cement will make the top.

To make this bench into an animal, choose one of the 14-inch-wide ends of the bench to be the "head" end. Nail a 24-inch 1 × 2 board to the center of the 14-inch board so it protrudes upwards from the top of the bench for a neck. Nail a 5-inch wood scrap to the top front of the neck for a head. For a tail, nail a 6-inch scrap 2 × 2 to protrude backwards from the center of the other 14-inch board. Or perhaps you'd prefer a two-headed bench!

Now wrap your frame with a layer of window screening. You should be able to find some junked window screens. Tin snips are good for cutting the screen into manageable pieces. A staple gun is a nice tool for fastening the screen to the wood frame, but tacks work well also. The screen should be stretched tightly over the top of the frame. It can be looser around the legs and neck depending on how wide or narrow you wish your creature's features to be. You needn't bother to put wire on the creature's underbelly, but be sure you wrap screen all around the legs.

Now you are ready for the chicken wire. One-inch mesh is preferable, but 2-inch mesh will work as well. I used about 30 feet of 18-inch-wide 1-inch mesh to complete this project. Staple or tack the chicken wire over the screening. The chicken wire provides reinforcement to the cement, so use extra layers at points of stress, such as where the legs and neck join the body. As much as possible, use large pieces of chicken wire to provide a continuous network of wire throughout the animal-bench. Cut wire to hold the chicken wire in place. If you are using the 2-inch mesh, a third layer of screening. Your cement will be forced into the spaces between the screening and the layers of chicken wire, giving you a strong ferro-cement. A 1-inch thickness of mortar is about ideal.

When the first layer of chicken wire is complete, cover the same surfaces with a second layer of wire mesh. If in places your wood frame becomes lost in the jungle of screen and chicken wire, you may twist pieces of ordinary wire to hold the chicken wire in place. If you are using the 2-inch mesh, a third layer of chicken wire is advisable. Bend any protruding sharp wire ends back into the interior of the bench creature, so they won't stick out of the finished bench or prick you as you trowel on the mortar.

Now you are ready to mix your mortar. You should mix only small batches at a time, trowelling each batch on before it hardens. An old bucket is large enough for mixing each batch. I found a small gardening trowel to be the most useful tool, both for mixing and applying the mortar. A cement trowel is handy also. Mix one part of masonry cement with two parts of clean sand for the mortar. A bag of premixed sand and cement would work well, too, though I'd recommend adding a little extra straight cement to the mix. Add only the minimum amount of water needed to make a very stiff mixture. Excess water results in a weaker final product. Trowel the mortar onto the surface of the creature, forcing the mortar through the chicken wire to the screening. In more difficult areas, such as the neck and legs, you will probably find it easier to take gobs of mortar and force them into the chicken wire with your hands. Mortar is rough on the hands, so rubber gloves are a good idea. For the strongest possible structure, allow yourself several hours to trowel on all the mortar at one time. You can also add to and patch up dried mortar.

62

Decorating your creature is a lot of the fun. Pieces of ceramic tile, broken mirror, and sea shells are among the many things that can be embedded into the still-moist mortar. Spread enough mortar over the top edges of these decorations to ensure that they will be held in place.

After the mortar has dried for one day, you can scrape or sand down the uneven surfaces. Allow two days' drying before moving or sitting on the animal-bench.

This is only one example of what you can make in ferro-cement. Using these techniques you could make all kinds of furniture, creatures, or small houses.

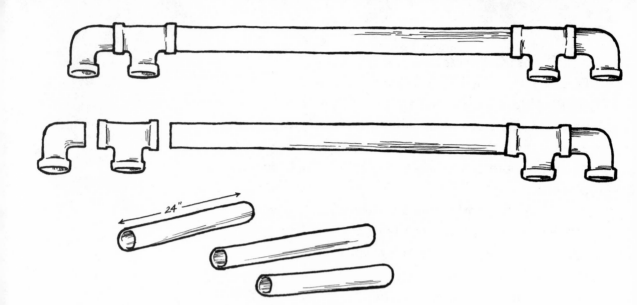

MOSQUITO TENT/TABLE

In planning this book I intended to include several projects constructed of hard plastic plumbing pipe (PVC) and pipe connectors. But when I went to purchase the necessary materials, I was discouraged by the price. If you have these materials or can afford them, the pipe and connectors are fun. Everything fits together easily and can be glued permanently with a glue manufactured for this purpose.

I include this one project because its value as camping equipment may justify your investment. The structure is strong, lightweight, and disassembles completely. It serves as a table and can be easily adapted into a mosquito or rain tent.

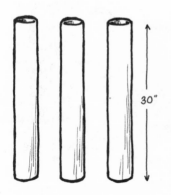

Cut the following pieces out of 1½-inch-diameter PVC pipe: four 30-inch lengths, two 2-foot lengths, and two 5½-foot lengths. (Don't use your favorite saw to cut the pipe as it will

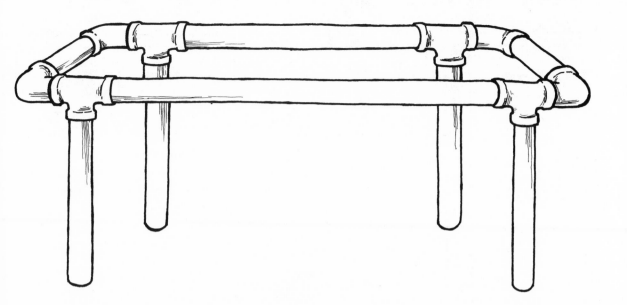

dull the saw.) Buy four 1½-inch **T**-connectors
and four 1½-inch 90-degree elbows. Elbows are
manufactured in two styles. Get the type illustrated, so one end will fit over the pipe end and
the other will fit inside the **T**-connector.

Attach a **T** to each end of the 5½-foot
pieces. Connect an elbow to the remaining end
of each **T**. Now connect the four elbows with
the two 2-foot pipes. To this rectangle attach
one 30-inch leg at each **T**. If the legs are splayed
every which way, rotate the **T**'s until all legs are
standing straight under the plane formed by the
pipe rectangle. For stability, the legs should be
pushed or dug a few inches into the ground.
The bottom of these pipes can be sawed to a
taper to make this easier, or they can be fitted
over stakes in the ground. The connectors
should all stay together pretty well; if they tend
to spread, you can stretch tight strings between
opposite pipes to pull them together.   **65**

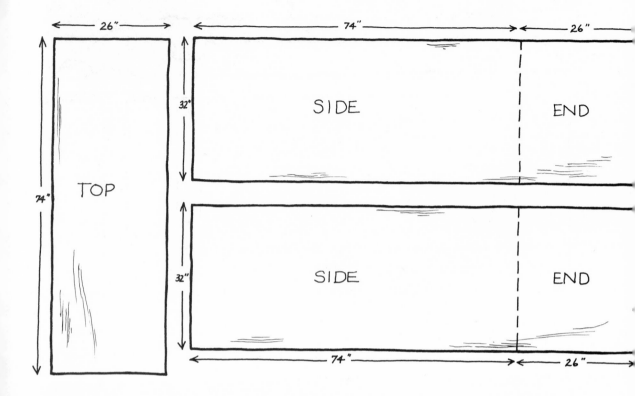

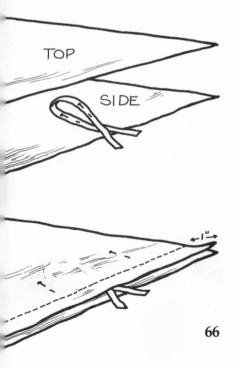

To use this frame for a table, place a piece of plywood or several boards across the top of the pipes. A few holes drilled through the table top above the horizontal pipes will allow you to loop a twine through the table and around the pipes to tie them together, securing the table top to the legs.

To use the framework for a mosquito tent, just hang a mosquito net from the pipes. This tent will be sleeping-bag size and should give you pleasant, biteless nights. Mosquito-net material is available from camping supply, surplus, and sometimes from fabric stores. Cut the pieces and sew them together as indicated in the diagram.

66

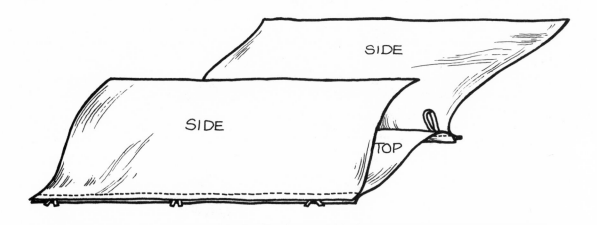

The two sides of the tent are rectangles 6 by 2½ feet. The two ends are 2 by 2½ feet, and the top is 2 by 6 feet. Allowing an extra inch on each edge of each piece for the seams and hem, you will need to cut two 74- by 32-inch pieces, two 26- by 32-inch pieces, and one 26- by 74-inch piece. As you sew, stitch one inch in from all edges for the seam allowance.

Sew one side to each side of the top along their 74-inch edges. Stick three folded 15-inch tapes or ribbons into each of these seams, one at each corner and one at the center. The diagram shows you how. It is by these tapes that the mosquito tent will hang from the pipe framework.

Next, sew the ends of the tent to the top along the 24-inch seams, leaving 1 inch of the tent ends free on each end of the seam. Sew the remaining four seams along the remaining 31-inch edges. Finish the bottom of the tent by enclosing it in double-fold bias tape and stitching through the tape and tent hem. Bias tape can be bought wherever sewing supplies are sold. It helps discourage ripping. **67**

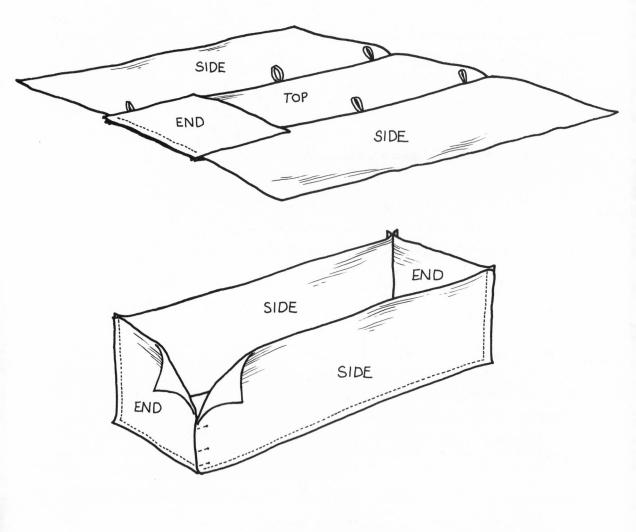

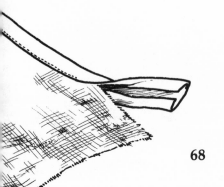

Your mosquito tent is now finished and can be hung inside the pipe frame by the tapes.

To turn the mosquito tent into a rudimentary rain tent, place the table top on top of the frame with the mosquito net below. For better protection, get an 8- by 8-foot tarp made of canvas, tent nylon, or polyethylene plastic. If your tarp has grommets in the corners, tie a 2-foot

68

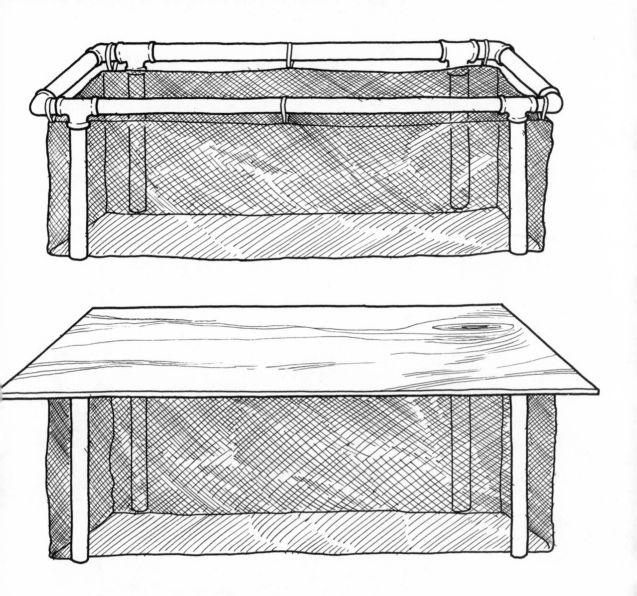

piece of twine through each of them. If not, you
can sew the twine into each corner. Another
trick is to find four pebbles and wrap one
into a 3-inch fold at each corner. Tie the twine
around the fold, holding the pebble in a little
sack. The pebble prevents the knot in the twine
from slipping off the corner of the tarp.

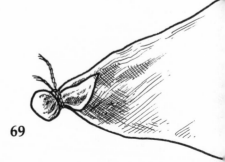

69

Spread the tarp over the top of the table as shown. Pound an 8-inch stake (wood, metal, or plastic) into the ground just outside each corner of the tarp. Tie each corner to the stakes, stretching the tarp taut. You can use the tarp without the table top, but I wouldn't want to be inside in a heavy rain with a pool of water above me. These pipes can be adapted to other tent frames.

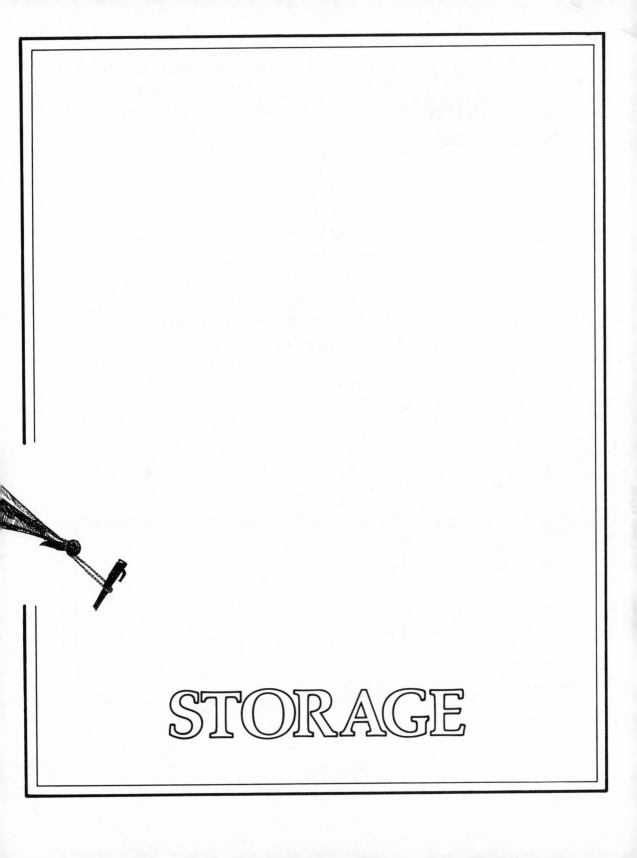

STORAGE

POCKET BANNER

The pocket banner is a large cloth rectangle (2½ by 5 feet is a good size) that hangs against the wall. Sew different sized pockets onto the banner to provide places to store such items as magazines, pencils, flashlights, hairbrushes, tools, or a pocket-size radio.

First, hem the cloth for the banner on all sides. Then, to make it hang smoothly, fold up the top and bottom 2½ inches of the banner. Sew down the fold with a line of stitches 2 inches from and parallel to the fold. This 2-inch section will provide a top and bottom casing through which you can insert wooden sticks or dowels. Tie a piece of twine to each end of the top stick for hanging. The stick in the bottom casing acts as a weight, keeping the banner smooth.

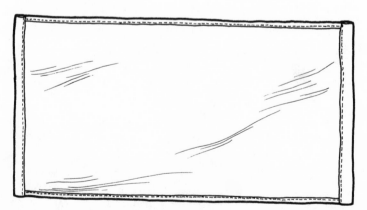

The banner's beauty depends upon your choice and arrangement of different fabrics for the pockets and background. You can treat the whole banner like a patchwork quilt made up of pockets, or even make needlework decorations on the banner.

ORNATE BOX-ON-THE-WALL

You can convert a sturdy cardboard box, such as a liquor carton, into a unique wall-storage cabinet. The box is mounted with the bottom against the wall. If you want a large storage space, use the whole box as one compartment; for small cubbyholes, leave the carton dividers in the box. Use the top box flaps as doors to the cabinet. Two flaps can meet in the center as double doors, or if three sides of the box top have been cut open, use the fourth side as a hinge to a single door.

A simple latch for the doors can be made with four large buttons and some strong thread. Make a small nail hole one inch from the edge of each door flap so that the two holes are next to each other when the doors are closed. (If you have a single door, make one on the door and one on the box side.) Sewing through the nail hole, put a button on the inside and outside of each hole. Tie a 1-foot piece of string around

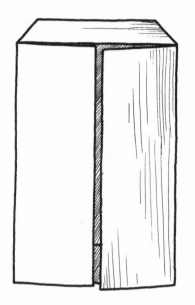

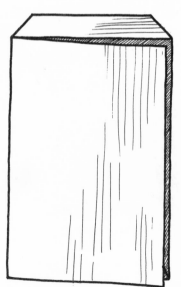

the button on the outside of one door. When you shut the doors, wrap the string several turns around the two buttons. The doors will stay tightly closed.

Although you could just mount your box on the wall at this point, there are many decorative possibilities for it and now is the time to consider them. How about a flower or a monster, a sun or an abstract pattern? You might decide to mount a mirror or a picture on the cupboard doors. My own suggestion would be to finish it with papier-maché and paint. Here's one example:

A "face" can be made by taping two paper cups to the box doors as eyes. Cut two pieces of corrugated cardboard in the shapes indicated, then fold and tape them in place on adjoining edges of the door flaps for two halves of a nose. Now cover this paper-cup-and-cardboard face with papier-maché.(Look back to the Tools and

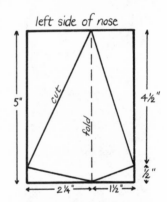

left side of nose

5"

cut

fold

4½"

½"

← 2¼" → ← 1½" →

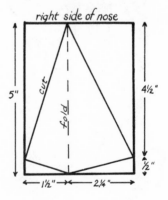

right side of nose

5"

cut

fold

4½"

½"

← 1½" → ← 2¼" →

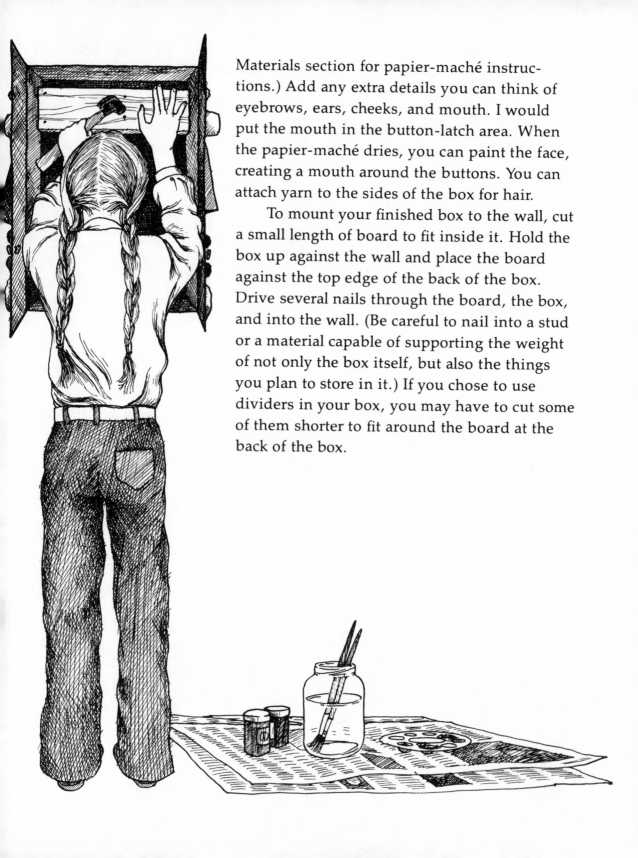

Materials section for papier-maché instructions.) Add any extra details you can think of eyebrows, ears, cheeks, and mouth. I would put the mouth in the button-latch area. When the papier-maché dries, you can paint the face, creating a mouth around the buttons. You can attach yarn to the sides of the box for hair.

To mount your finished box to the wall, cut a small length of board to fit inside it. Hold the box up against the wall and place the board against the top edge of the back of the box. Drive several nails through the board, the box, and into the wall. (Be careful to nail into a stud or a material capable of supporting the weight of not only the box itself, but also the things you plan to store in it.) If you chose to use dividers in your box, you may have to cut some of them shorter to fit around the board at the back of the box.

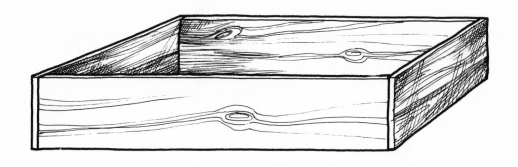

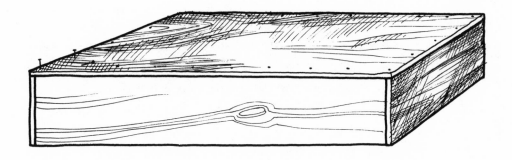

This is a tidy way to hide a lot of junk under your bed. It is simply a wooden box with furniture casters on the bottom to help it roll easily in and out.

You will need two 22-inch and two 32-inch planed ¾- by 6-inch boards for the box sides, and a 22- by 33½-inch rectangle of ⅜- or ½-inch plywood for the bottom. You will also need eight 1½-inch flathead screws, twenty 1¼-inch nails, four furniture casters of a type that will screw to the bottom of a box, and the necessary screws to attach the casters.

Arrange the four boards in a box shape so that the plywood fits exactly on top of them, the outer edges of the boards precisely meeting the

UNDER-BED ROLLING BOX

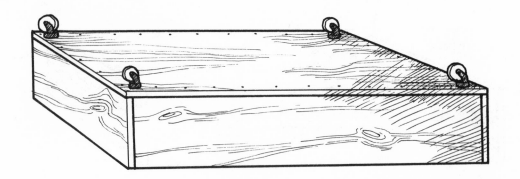

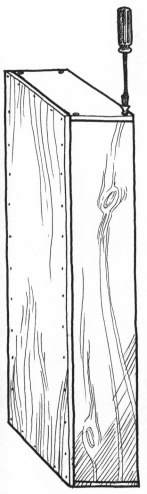

outer edges of the plywood. Nail through the plywood into the boards. Now, with the bottom firmly attached to the sides of the box, turn it over and screw the sides to one another, using two screws per corner. Drill small holes to guide the screws, and larger shallow holes to provide a recess, so that the flathead screws will be flush with the sides. Turn the box upside down again and screw a caster to each corner of the plywood bottom.

Your box is complete. You can paint it or add a handle. Three boxes will fit under an average bed, or you can make boxes of different dimensions.

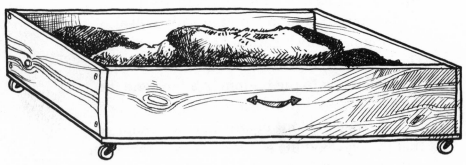

This stool serves as both a seat and a storage container. It is made of a 15-inch section of 10- or 12-inch-diameter fiber tube. For more information on fiber tubing look back to the Fiber-Tube Desk project.

In addition to the 15-inch fiber tube, you'll need to cut three disks out of wide board or plywood. One disk is made by standing the tube on top of the wood and drawing around the *outside* circumference of the tube onto the wood. Cut this disk out with a jigsaw. The other two disks are drawn from the *inside* of the tube for the inside circumference. Cut out these disks.

STORAGE
STOOL

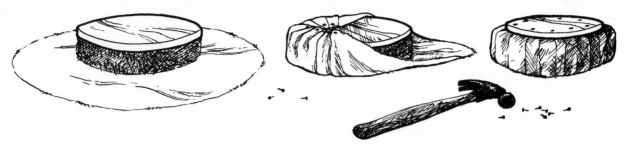

Place one of the smaller disks inside the bottom of the tube. Nail through the sides of the tube into the edges of the wood disk to attach the bottom.

To make the cushioned stool top, cut a 2-inch-thick circle of foam rubber the size of the larger disk. Cut out a round piece of cloth with a diameter 8 inches wider than that of the disk. Place the foam rubber on top of the cloth and the larger disk on top of the foam. Wrap the cloth over the foam and plywood and tack it to the underside (the underside is up in this position) of the disk.

Center the remaining wood disk on the underside of the cushioned disk and nail it in place with 1-inch or shorter nails. This smaller disk should fit inside the tube while the larger one rests on top, making a snug-fitting, removable top to your storage stool.

It's fun to decorate the tube with a collage, paint, or cloth.

NEW

SPACES

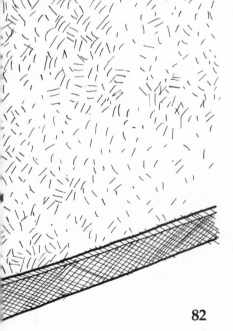

BILLOWING-CLOUD CEILING

The billowing-cloud ceiling is a purely decorative way to change the feeling of your room. It provides a soft cloud-like effect, and also diffuses any overhead lighting. The billowing-cloud ceiling is achieved by making a grid of taut fishing line below and parallel to the ceiling. Very lightweight cloth (a surplus silk parachute is ideal) is spread on top of the grid and will sag down between the fishing lines.

The fishing lines will be attached to screw eyes fastened to the top of the walls at a distance of a few inches from the ceiling. CAUTION: *If you have a ceiling light fixture, increase the distance from the ceiling to avoid a fire hazard.* If you have molding around the ceiling, fasten the screw eyes into it. However, even Sheetrock walls should be able to support the moderate stress from the cloud ceiling, providing you don't hang too many other items from it. Space the screw eyes 2 feet apart around all four walls of the room. If your room is an irregular shape (not square or rectangular), you will have to calculate the spacing to get a perfect grid. But

82

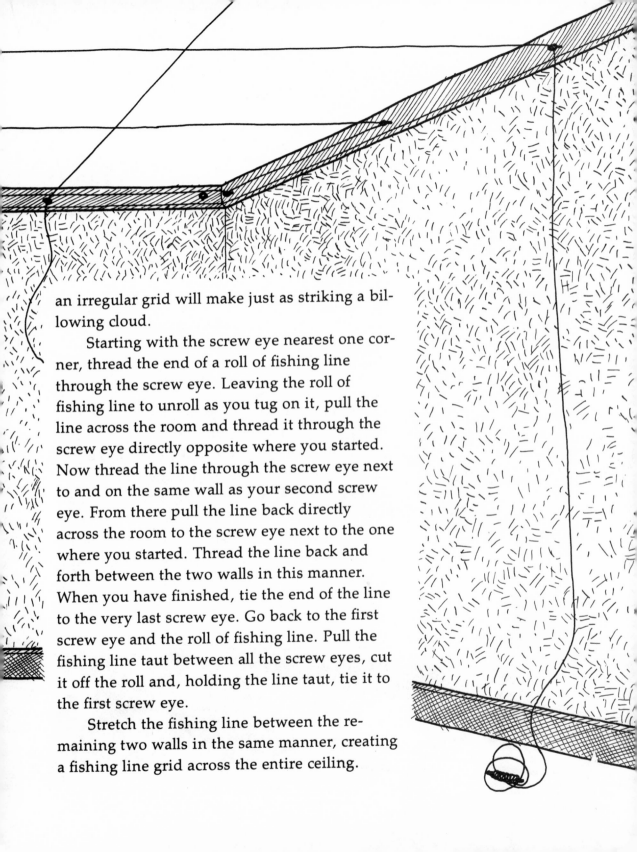

an irregular grid will make just as striking a billowing cloud.

Starting with the screw eye nearest one corner, thread the end of a roll of fishing line through the screw eye. Leaving the roll of fishing line to unroll as you tug on it, pull the line across the room and thread it through the screw eye directly opposite where you started. Now thread the line through the screw eye next to and on the same wall as your second screw eye. From there pull the line back directly across the room to the screw eye next to the one where you started. Thread the line back and forth between the two walls in this manner. When you have finished, tie the end of the line to the very last screw eye. Go back to the first screw eye and the roll of fishing line. Pull the fishing line taut between all the screw eyes, cut it off the roll and, holding the line taut, tie it to the first screw eye.

Stretch the fishing line between the remaining two walls in the same manner, creating a fishing line grid across the entire ceiling.

Spread your cloth over the top of the grid. A few safety pins here and there may be handy to hold the cloth in place. If the room has overhead lighting, it will look nice shining through the cloth clouds, but please be certain any light bulbs are *at least 6 inches from the cloth.* You can hang lightweight decorations such as mobiles or model planes from the fishing lines beneath the clouds.

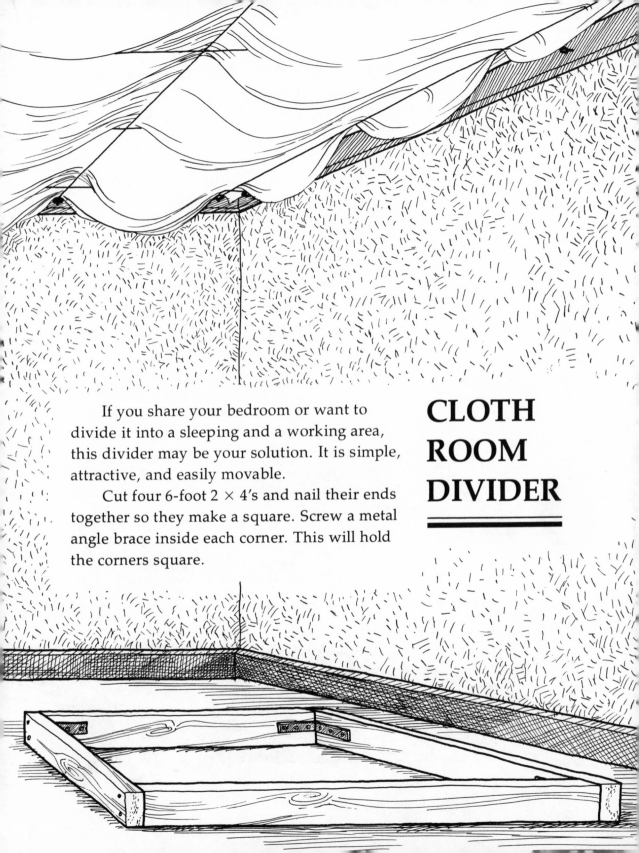

If you share your bedroom or want to divide it into a sleeping and a working area, this divider may be your solution. It is simple, attractive, and easily movable.

Cut four 6-foot 2 × 4's and nail their ends together so they make a square. Screw a metal angle brace inside each corner. This will hold the corners square.

CLOTH ROOM DIVIDER

Cut or sew cloth into a 7- by 7-foot square.
Lay it down flat on the floor. If the cloth has a
"right" side, place that side face down. Lay the
6- by 6-foot frame down on the cloth, so that
6 inches of cloth extend around all sides.

Starting in the center of one side, fold the
cloth around the 2 × 4 and staple or tack it once
to the back. Now cross to the opposite side of
the frame. Pull the cloth tightly and staple it to
the center of the back of that 2 × 4. Your third
staple will be in the center of the back of a perpendicular 2 × 4 and the fourth staple in the
2 × 4 opposite the third.

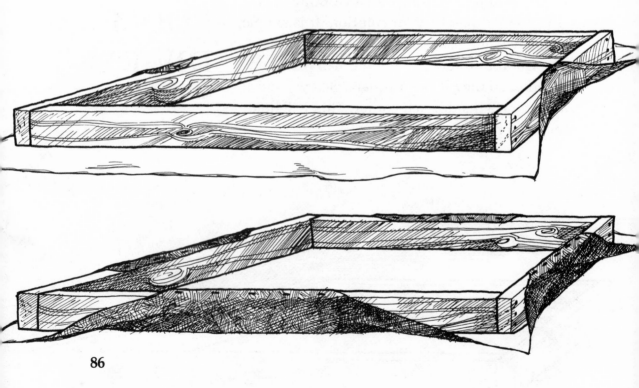

With all four centers stapled, proceed in the same order, adding one staple, then its opposite, working out from the center toward the corners. Staples should be spaced 3 inches apart. Try to apply an even tension to the cloth each time you staple.

At the corners, fold the cloth under (like a well-made bed or wrapped present) and staple it in position. You should now have a taut cloth panel. You may hang this divider from two screw eyes placed in the top 2 × 4 or support it from the floor by nailing a 2-foot board to the sides of the base of the two 2 × 4 uprights.

STORAGE-TUBE PARTITION

This storage unit consists of tubes laid on their sides to form compartments. You can use tubes of all sizes and materials in any combination. Some possibilities are short pieces of cardboard fiber tubes (manufactured as disposable concrete forms), tin cans with the top and/or bottom removed, mailing tubes, paper barrels, oatmeal boxes, ceramic pipe, large plastic pipe, or any other cylindrical container big enough to put something in. The tubes should be of approximately the same length. A good length for most uses is 8 or 10 inches, though long tubes are handy for storing large rolled-up papers.

Build a square or rectangular frame out of 1 × 8's. The length of the boards will vary according to your desired unit size. Keep in mind that it takes many tubes to fill a large partition. The frame acts as an enclosure to prevent the stacked tubes from rolling away. Attach metal angle braces to the corners for added strength and fill the frame with tubes, fitting them in as tightly as possible.

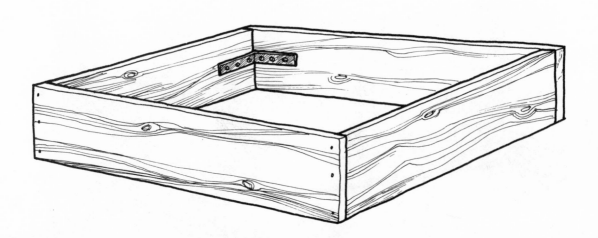

If the tubes slip around, add some extra small tubes to tighten the fit, or glue the frame and tubes together.

Use this tube-storage structure against a wall or as a partition accessible from both sides. If you have chosen large tubes, you can cut some shelves the width of the inside diameters and fit them through the middle of the tubes.

BOOKSHELF PARTITIONS

Here are three methods of supporting bookshelves either against the wall or as free-standing partitions. Each method may be used alone or combined with the others. For shelves, use boards approximately 9 inches wide. If your shelves run longer than 4 feet, the first two construction methods will require a central support.

TIN-CAN SUPPORTS

These are simple enough: tin cans on end as spacers between the shelves. Tall fruit-juice cans are particularly suited for most book heights. Tuna-fish cans are a good height to raise the bottom shelf off the floor. You can fill the cans with sand for greater stability. Rather than cans you could use strong tubes made of cardboard or other materials.

TRIANGULAR TUBE SUPPORTS

Make a triangular tube support out of a 24- by 8-inch piece of corrugated cardboard. The corrugations should run parallel to the 8-inch edges of the cardboard. Measure the cardboard so that the piece divides into three equal squares. Fold at the junctions between the squares. Firmly tape the loose ends together, creating a triangular cardboard tube.

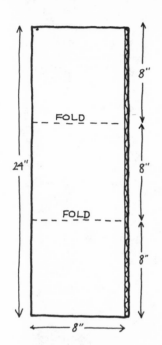

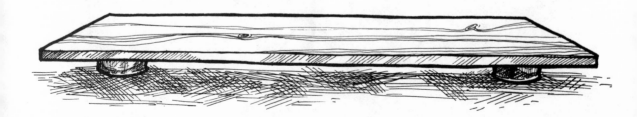

Place a triangular tube under each end of the shelf. A larger triangular tube could support a table or stool.

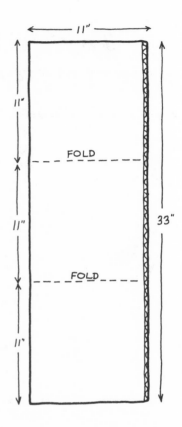

ZIG-ZAG SUPPORTS These are particularly appropriate to a shelf divider because the zig-zag pattern creates a series of triangular display compartments on both sides of the shelf.

Cut strips of corrugated cardboard 11 inches high with the corrugations running parallel to this edge. The length is optional but must be a multiple of 11 inches. Mark 11-inch squares on the strips and fold the cardboard in alternating directions at the junctions between the squares, making a zig-zag. You will probably need to tape several of these zig-zag strips together for a long shelf.

DRAGON DEN

This is a rather ambitious project—a giant dragon with a bed built on its back, a bookcase in its head, a private room underneath, and a tail to hang your clothes on! To build the basic structure you will need the following:

two 5-foot 1 × 4's	two 4-foot 2 × 4's
four 6-foot 1 × 4's	four 5-foot 2 × 4's
two 9-foot 1 × 4's	two 8-foot 2 × 4's
two 21-inch 2 × 4's	one 14-foot 2 × 4
one sheet of ⅝-inch (or thicker) plywood	

Nail the two 8-foot 2 × 4's under the two 8-foot edges of the plywood. Nail the 14-foot 2 × 4 parallel to the 8-footers down the center of the plywood so that one end extends 2 feet beyond the edge of the plywood and the other end extends 4 feet beyond the opposite edge of the plywood.

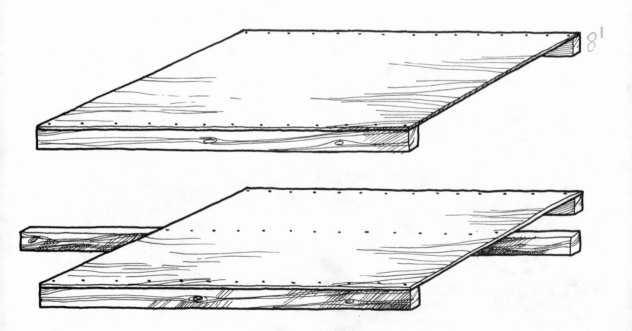

8'

At the 4-feet-wide edges of the plywood, nail the 21-inch 2 × 4's perpendicular to and between the long 2 × 4's. IMPORTANT: If you are using planed 2 × 4's, their true thickness is probably less than 2 inches; in this case you'll need to cut these strips slightly longer than 21 inches. Measure carefully.

With the 2 × 4 supports nailed under the plywood, you are ready to attach the legs. To do so, the plywood should be placed on the floor with the 2 × 4 supports facing up. Nail one of the 5-foot 2 × 4 legs to the 2 × 4 supports inside each corner of the plywood. Check these legs with a carpenter's square to make absolutely sure that they are at 90-degree angles to the plywood.

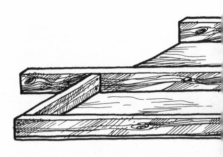

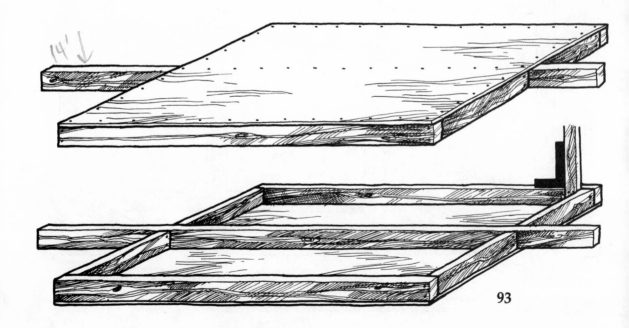

At each of the 4-foot ends of the plywood, nail a 4-foot 2 × 4 between the legs so it rests directly on top of the two 21-inch 2 × 4 supports. When turned over, these 4-foot 2 × 4's will prevent the plywood from sagging in the middle.

As you can see in the illustrations, you need braces between the legs to make them firm. On the three sides where there are **X** braces, one 1 × 4 can be nailed to the inside of the legs and the other to the outside. The 9-foot 1 × 4's are for one of the 8-foot sides of the dragon. On the other 8-foot side, you nail two 5-foot triangular braces so as to leave an opening to get under the bed.

With all these 2 × 4's and braces nailed together, the essential structure is complete. Get

some help turning it over so that it stands on its legs. You could use this "as is" with a mattress on top and a desk below. But having done the hard work, why not enjoy the fun of turning it into a dragon?

The portions of 2 × 4 extending beyond the ends of the plywood are the beginnings of the head and tail. The 2-foot extension is the framework of the dragon's bottom jaw. Nail a 2-foot board to the side of this 2 × 4 to create a **V** shape. The wider the **V,** the farther open the dragon's mouth. Attach a sturdy cardboard or wooden box on top of the plywood, centered over the mouth framework. This box will form the framework for the rest of the head. The back of the box can be left open as a bookcase or storage area accessible from the bed.

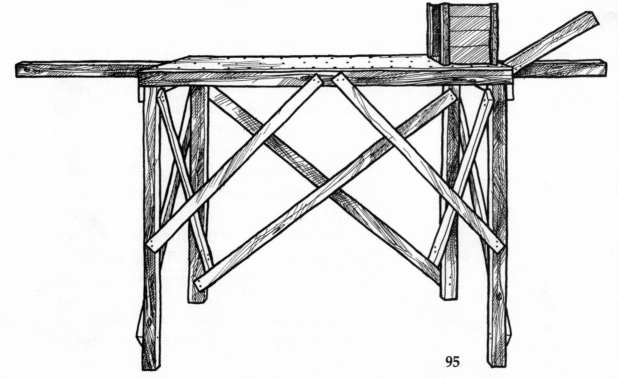

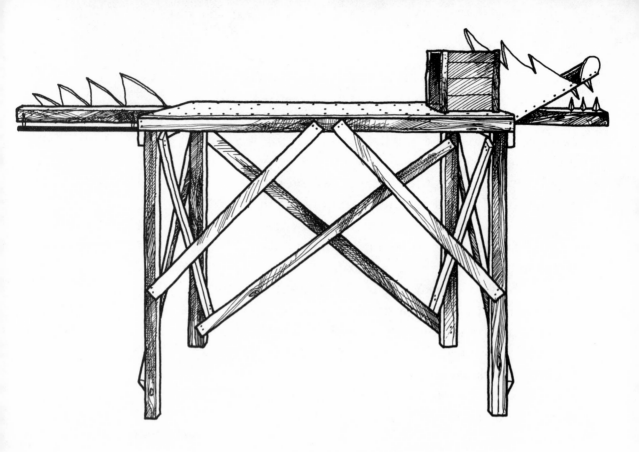

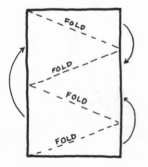

Attach cardboard between the box and the
jaws, completing a framework for the dragon's
papier-maché head. Teeth can be made by folding thin cardboard into tetrahedrons (see detail)
and taping them to the insides of the mouth.
Papier-maché the whole head, following the
method described in the Tools and Materials
section.

The 4-foot 2 × 4 extending from the rear of
the dragon will become its tail. Tack or staple
pieces of corrugated cardboard to the top of this
2 × 4 to make it look like a jagged tail. The tail
also serves as a closet. Hang a 4-foot length of
metal water pipe by wire several inches below

the 2 × 4 tail. You can hang clothes hangers on
this pipe or papier-maché the tail.

When the papier-maché is dry, paint the
head and tail in "dragonesque" colors.

Now comes the task of putting sides on the
large body. If you have lots of large cardboard,
you could tack it to the structure and paint it.
Another solution is to thumbtack cloth to hang
around all four sides of the body. The side
without an **X**-brace between the legs allows you
to part the cloth curtains and enter your private
room inside the dragon. Put a mattress on top
of the dragon's back and you can go to sleep in
style.

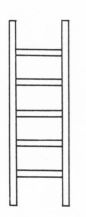

You may now want to build a ladder. Start by laying two parallel 6-foot 2 × 4's 18 inches apart. Cut five 18-inch 2 × 2's for rungs and nail them between the 6-foot 2 × 4's at 1-foot intervals. Stand this ladder against the bed platform at a comfortable angle. Now nail an 18-inch 1 × 3 to the back of the ladder just above the point where it touches the platform. In addition to strengthening the ladder, this 1 × 3 will prevent it from slipping away when you put **98** your weight on it.

LAMPS AND

ACCESSORIES

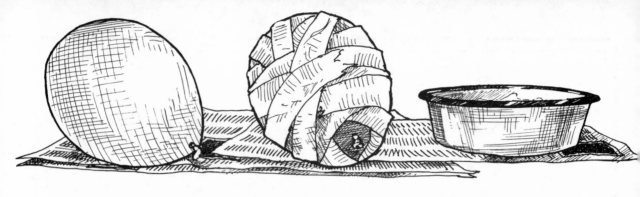

PAPIER-MACHÉ BALLOON LAMPSHADE

In this project you turn a balloon into a lampshade!

Inflate a balloon just a bit larger than the size you want your lampshade to be and make sure it's securely tied off. Cover the balloon with at least three layers of papier-maché. (Consult the Tools and Materials section, p.8, for papier-maché directions.) After the papier-maché is hard, you can burst the balloon with a pin.

When you attach a papier-maché lampshade to a light bulb it is absolutely critical to leave plenty of space between the bulb and the paper, or it could catch fire! To ensure a really safe distance, use the fitting from an old broken lampshade. If you can't find an old lampshade, you can buy these fittings from hardware, lighting, or craft stores.

The most common fitting consists of two circles of wire that clamp around the bulb. This clamp connects to a wire ring that frames the top of the lampshade. Study the old lampshade for a few minutes; you will attach your papier-maché shade in the same manner. In one end of the balloon shape, cut a hole the same diameter as the ring of the old lampshade. Tape, glue, sew, wire, or papier-maché the paper balloon to the wire ring of the fitting. Cut a hole in the other end of the papier-maché shell; the size of this hole will depend upon the lamp to which you attach the shade.

For different effects, experiment with different color papers or the color-comic pages of a newspaper.

CORRUGATED LAMPSHADE

This lampshade consists of donut-shaped pieces of corrugated cardboard stacked in diminishing size to form a conical shape. Light will show through the corrugations as well as through the donut hole.

Draw out the "donut rings" on cardboard with a compass, then cut them out with a narrow-tip, razor-blade knife. If you want to be really professional about it, you can buy a compass with a cutter-blade attachment. The

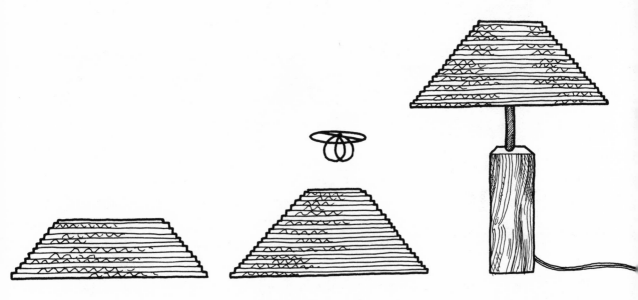

donuts can be as big as you want, but the space
between the hole and the outer edge should be
at least 2 inches wide. The inside and the outside radius of each donut ring should be
slightly smaller than those of the one before.

Use the same type of bulb fitting as we rec-
ommended in the papier-maché balloon
lampshade project. The interior radius of the
top donut ring should measure ¼ inch less than
the radius of the ring on the bulb fitting. The
lampshade will then sit on top of the wire ring.
Punch a few nail holes near the inside ring of
the top piece of cardboard. Tie thin wire
through these holes and around the wire ring to
fasten them together.

This conical lampshade is just a start. Using the same technique, you can just as easily
design a square, rectangular, cylindrical,
pyramidal, or free-form shade.

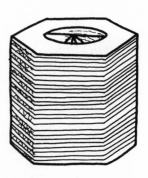

LAMPSHADE
OF STICKS

This lampshade is of "log-cabin" construction and can be created from popsicle sticks, wood strips, twigs, or branches. If you use twigs, flatten the ends with a jackknife so they'll lie flat on top of one another. Start with two parallel sticks. Glue two more parallel sticks between them. Keep building up this square-base lampshade in this manner.

You can wire the shade to a bulb clamp as in the previous lampshade projects, or you can build a shade tall enough to rest on a table and surround both the bulb and its base. You can make any straight-sided shape using this construction. Try a triangle, pentagon, hexagon, or pyramid. By altering the lengths of your sticks you can even make bulging shapes.

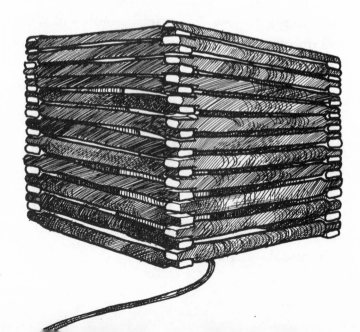

Tin cans make great lamps and lampshades. I used large cans 6 inches in diameter and 7 inches high. (These can often be salvaged from school cafeterias.) However, a variety of sizes will work.

The essential elements of these lamps are the light fixtures available inexpensively at a hardware store. The kind you want is designed so that a hollow ⅜-inch-diameter threaded rod screws into the base of the fitting. A nut screws onto the other end of this threaded rod. You feed the rod through a ⅜-inch hole in the can, then screw on the nut, holding the can tightly to the fixture. A 1½-inch-long threaded rod is adequate for these projects, but much longer rods are available if you want to try variations. The electric wire passes through the middle of the hollow rod.

TIN-CAN LAMPS

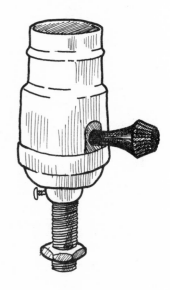

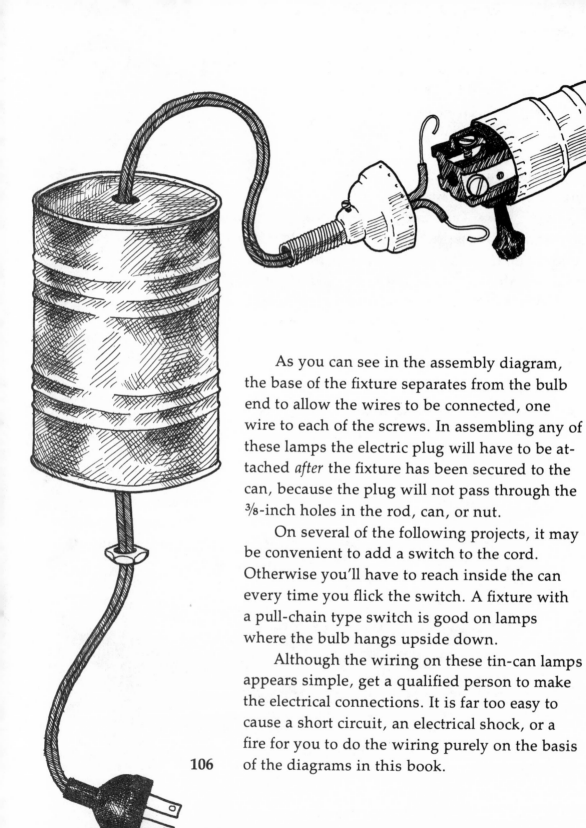

As you can see in the assembly diagram, the base of the fixture separates from the bulb end to allow the wires to be connected, one wire to each of the screws. In assembling any of these lamps the electric plug will have to be attached *after* the fixture has been secured to the can, because the plug will not pass through the ⅜-inch holes in the rod, can, or nut.

On several of the following projects, it may be convenient to add a switch to the cord. Otherwise you'll have to reach inside the can every time you flick the switch. A fixture with a pull-chain type switch is good on lamps where the bulb hangs upside down.

Although the wiring on these tin-can lamps appears simple, get a qualified person to make the electrical connections. It is far too easy to cause a short circuit, an electrical shock, or a fire for you to do the wiring purely on the basis of the diagrams in this book.

106

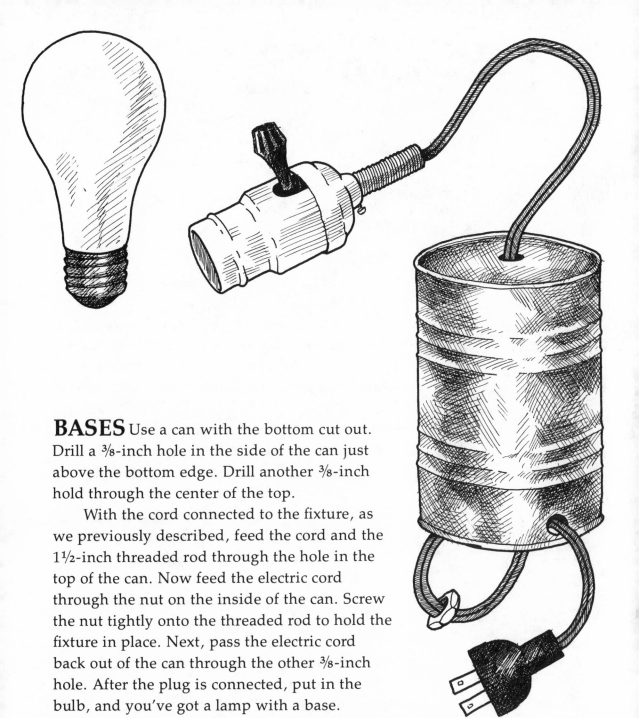

BASES Use a can with the bottom cut out. Drill a ⅜-inch hole in the side of the can just above the bottom edge. Drill another ⅜-inch hold through the center of the top.

With the cord connected to the fixture, as we previously described, feed the cord and the 1½-inch threaded rod through the hole in the top of the can. Now feed the electric cord through the nut on the inside of the can. Screw the nut tightly onto the threaded rod to hold the fixture in place. Next, pass the electric cord back out of the can through the other ⅜-inch hole. After the plug is connected, put in the bulb, and you've got a lamp with a base.

You can use a conventional lampshade, one of the shades from an earlier project, or a tin-can lampshade.

107

SHADES Remove the top from a can and drill a ⅜-inch hole in the center of the bottom. Take apart and reassemble the lamp base so that the threaded rod passes through the bottom of both cans, holding them together. When the switch is turned on, light will come from the top of the shade.

A wall lamp can be made using this same can shade and fixture without the base. Drill two small holes in the side of the can—one near the top, the other near the bottom. Hammer a nail into the wall (be sure to locate a stud) and hang the can lamp from it. You'll be able to direct the light up or down, depending on which hole you hang the lamp from.

To make a wall lamp that directs the light *across* the room, drill a ⅜-inch hole in the center of the can side. Make a hole in the bottom of the can to hang it from and put a hook or nail into the wall where you want the lamp to be. Hang the can on the wall with the ⅜-inch hole facing down. Attach the fixture through this hole. You can use this as a ceiling lamp by screwing the can bottom to the ceiling.

These tin-can shades direct all the light out through one end of the can. You can create more interesting lampshades and light patterns by punching designs into the cans. Perhaps you have seen some of the fine Mexican tincraft that's made this way. These puncture holes also serve to ventilate the lampshades, preventing heat buildup. The easiest method is to puncture the designs by hammering nails of various sizes through the tin. To avoid crumpling the can in the process of decorating, you need something inside the can to hammer against. The easiest solution is to mount a small log in a vise (or clamp it to a work table) so that the end of the log protrudes. Slip the can over the end of the log and nail through the tin. You can also drill, snip, or saw designs into the can. Parallel strips cut up the sides of the can and curled give a fringed effect, but be careful not to cut yourself on the sharp edges.

PIVOT DESK LAMP

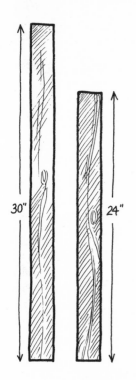

30"   24"

This pivot desk lamp uses the same type of fixture and tin-can shade with a ⅜-inch hole drilled in the center of the bottom, as we've described in previous projects. However, this lamp is mounted on an adjustable stand that you can clamp or nail to a desk, table, or workbench.

The stand is made of two 2 × 2's: one 24 inches long and one 30 inches long. Place the 2 × 2's on top of each other so that they meet at one end. From that end, measure in 2 inches and drill a centered hole through both 2 × 2's. Bolt them together with a nut and bolt so that they pivot tightly.

At the other end of the 24-inch 2 × 2, cut a taper parallel to the bolt extending 1 foot and tapering to ½-inch thick at the point. Measuring in 4 inches from the taper point, drill a centered ⅜-inch hole through the tapered section. This hole is at a perpendicular angle to the pivot hole. Feed the cord and threaded rod through this hole and fasten the nut, completing the lamp as illustrated. Nail or screw the base of the 30-inch 2 × 2 into the side of your desk or workbench to make it stand upright.

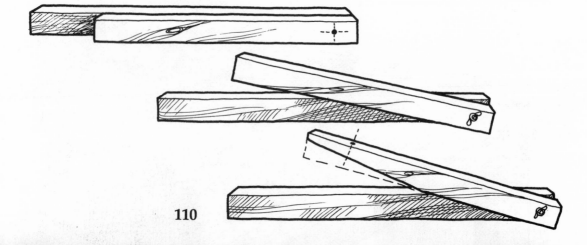

If your desk is thin-topped without sides, attach an extra block of wood to the underside of the desk top and mount the lamp on this block.

You can refine this design by attaching the upright 2 × 2 to the desk with a hinge, rather than with nails or screws. You will then be able to adjust the lamp forward and back in addition to pivoting it up and down.

Use a few U-shaped nails to loosely attach the electric cord to the 2 × 2's.

PATCHWORK RUG

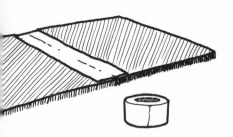

Rug companies make square or rectangular samples of their carpets and often discard them or sell them very inexpensively after a design has gone out of production. If you can get hold of a number of these squares, they will make a great patchwork rug! Tape the backs of the squares together using a 3″-wide masking tape. You can also cut the scraps into interesting designs and tape them together that way.

Another good source of carpet pieces for your patchwork rug is old carpets, which are often thrown away because of staining or uneven wear. Cut the good sections out with a utility knife and use them in the patchwork rug.

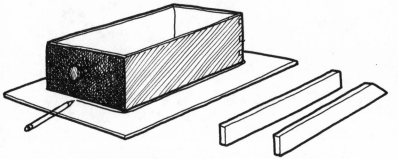

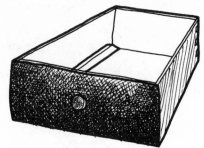

I have an old writing box of my great-grandmother's that contains a secret hiding place. Have you ever wanted a secret place to conceal your papers or valuables? A false bottom in a drawer or box is an excellent way to hide things from a nosy brother or sister.

Cut a piece of thin plywood the exact size of the inside of your drawer or box. This plywood will be the false bottom.

Cut two 1/2- by 1 1/2-inch wood strips the length of the drawer interior. Draw a line on the flat side of each strip at an angle 45 degrees from one corner. Cut off the end of each strip along this line. Now glue these strips to the sides of the drawer along the bottom inside edge, with the 45-degree-cut edge facing up at the back of the drawer. Attach another 1/2- by 1 1/2-inch strip along the bottom front edge, between the side strips. Place the plywood false bottom in the drawer, resting it on the strips. To get at this secret 1 1/2-inch space, press the false bottom at the back of the drawer and the front will pop up. You can make the 1 1/2-inch height of the secret compartment greater or smaller depending on the depth of your drawer or box.

FALSE-BOTTOM DRAWER OR BOX

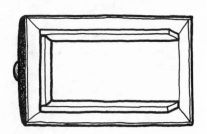

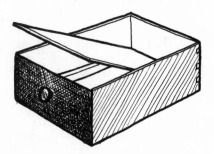

113

COLORED-GLASS WINDOWS

To create a stained-glass effect on your windows, try this: Rub some Vaseline on the glass; then cut out pieces of colored tissue-paper and press them onto the Vaseline. Because the Vaseline doesn't dry, it will hold the paper in place. If you tire of your first design, just pull the paper off and press on a new one—try crinkling the tissue for a textured surface. When you no longer want a stained-glass window, wash off the Vaseline with soap and warm water.

ABOUT THE AUTHOR

Timothy Wilcox Fisher grew up in the United States, Ethiopia, Rhodesia, Malawi and Uganda. By the seventh grade he had attended nine different schools. At Putney School in Vermont he worked on sculpture and furniture making at the expense of his other courses. After apprenticing to a furniture maker and traveling in Africa and the Pacific, he earned a BFA in architecture at the Rhode Island School of Design. He now lives in northern Vermont with his wife, Kathleen Kolb, whom he married while they were both working on an earlier Addison-Wesley book, *Huts, Hovels & Houses*.

ABOUT THE ARTIST

Kathleen Kolb grew up in Ohio where from the age of six she took advantage of Saturday classes at the Cleveland Art Museum and later at the Cleveland Institute of Art. She earned her BFA in Illustration from the Rhode Island School of Design. Ms. Kolb is the oldest of six children, the rest of whom live in Florida where her parents also reside.